Lost Poetry of Los Angeles, 2011-2023

Praise for the poems of
"Lost Poetry of Los Angeles, 2011-2023"

"How did you know that thing about my brother?
I didn't even tell you that!"
- Poetry customer, Los Angeles Arts District, December 2021

"I love you."
- Poetry customer, Burbank, Mother's Day 2023

"Bro, you don't even understand:
you just saved me for Valentine's Day."
- Poetry customer, Los Angeles Arts District, February 2020

"That certainly is ... a poem."
- Poetry customer, Pasadena, July 2017

"When I arrived to my office this morning, your envelope
was waiting for me ... it is PERFECTION!"
- Poetry customer at work, Los Angeles, December 2022

Lost Poetry of Los Angeles,

2011-2023

*Stories abandoned
on the sidewalks of
Southern California,
and other poems*

By Bryan Mahoney

Edited by Marcy Mahoney, @marcy_mahoney on Instagram
Book and cover design by Bryan Mahoney, @the_typin_pint
www.thetypinpint.com

All fonts are licensed by Adobe.
Cover text and inside title: Broadsheet
Headers: Archetype
Body text: Baskerville URW

ISBN: 979-8-9899823-0-1

Second Edition: January 2024

10 9 8 7 6 5 4 3 2

For Marge

Every love poem
is for you

Especially
the weird ones

What you're about to read is a first draft. In most cases, the only draft. There are smudges. There are letters toppling over each other like they're pouring out of a spin cycle. When I think of how these stories come to me, the words rattling about my subconscious and collecting like static onto old socks … they're a physical representation of the art I poured into them. They are imperfect stories drummed out on a perfect little metal and glass and rubber machine.

The premise is straightforward: I talk to people for a couple minutes about their family, their friends, their job, their favorite vacation spots … anything they want me to write a poem about. Then they leave me to write five or six (usually) rhyming stanzas. I'll read the finished product to them then hand it over; they just have to come back in about 15 minutes.

Except sometimes they don't.

Sometimes people just forget they asked me for a poem. They get busy, or distracted, or maybe they have second thoughts about hearing what I've written. I wrote their poem anyway. I carried it in my leather satchel next to my notebooks and ink ribbons. If this was you, I had hoped to meet you one day and give it to you.

Hopefully you find this book and you remember, "Oh yeah – I did ask that guy to write me a poem about a wrestling match in a forest."

Over the years, people have shared extremely personal stories with me. I've been asked to write obituaries for long missed friends, love poems for desperate partners, and wish fulfillments for parents hoping their children will become surgeons, leaders, and astronaut monster truck drivers.

In the summer of 2022, I was interviewed by the L.A. Daily News about my street poems. A photographer and I sat on a Burbank sidewalk outside an oddities museum and a vintage clothing store. We waited for hours and I got only one request – two friends, Daniela and Courtney, who wanted a poem about UFOs and their adventures with extraterrestrials. Then they went away.

I wrote. The photographer took photos.

The friends never returned.

"What do you do if they don't come back?" the photojournalist asked me as we waited for another subject that would never come.

A year later, this is my answer.

section 1

Lost Poetry

poems written for people who left their poem behind

BRYAN MAHONEY

The Aliens Are Us

The air was quite crisp on a Thursday
Daniela was thankful for shades
The sun beat a sharp shard of brightness
Attacking her eyeballs like blades

But walking in Burbank was pleasant
Until something covered the sun
Daniela looked up at a spaceship
A saucer, for sure, built for one.

And flying the starcraft was Courtney
"Come on," her friend said, "and let's go
She landed and picked up Daniela
But where should they fly? I don't know.

The ship picked up speed over Burbank
The readout said nineteen-sixty
So Courtney hit Start on the console
Just in time before hitting a tree.

The saucer blinked out of existence
And popped into air in the past
The girls were surrounded by mod clothes
And other old styles not to last.

"So cool!" said Daniela, 'pon leaving
And Courtney soon followed her friend.
The people around them ran screaming;
They thought that the world was at end.

@ The Typin' PINT

They called the game "The Shredder"
It had another name
It got its reputation
From making gamers tame

Til one night in South Cali
A tournament arcade
Had met its match named Jackie
The Shredder dne got played.

She mastered all the buttons
And angled ɓr a win
A man approached from NASA
And asked if she was in.

They had a special mission
And Jackie hadtheskills
And Jeff joined her for training
(The mission paid their bills)

Amartian threat ɯs looming
They blasted into space
So Jackie ran ɦe lasers
For impact they did brace

The Martians fired boulders
Like city bɩocks and more
But Jackie aimed the laser
And blasted twenty-four

The pair staved off invasion
Parades were held for days
And Jackie's at the games now
'Cause savingEarth does pay.

section 1   lost poetry

BRYAN MAHONEY

The thing about the Troubles
They show up when they will
They eat up all your chutzpah
bThey sap up thoughts like swill

The Troubles whisper something
Too low and soft to hear
n Your body still responding
In doubt, and woe, and fear.

Insidious, they're creeping
The voices won't relent
They offer an instruction:
Obey or else repent

I ask them of my sinning
For what must I atone?
Is blame and guilt around me?
And why must I, alone?

The Troubles point a finger
A long thin reed of shame
They slowly whisper something
The breath carries my name

I sit here in my study
My mind gives way to waste
The troubles come to claim it
But find I'm not their taste,

The Typh' Pint

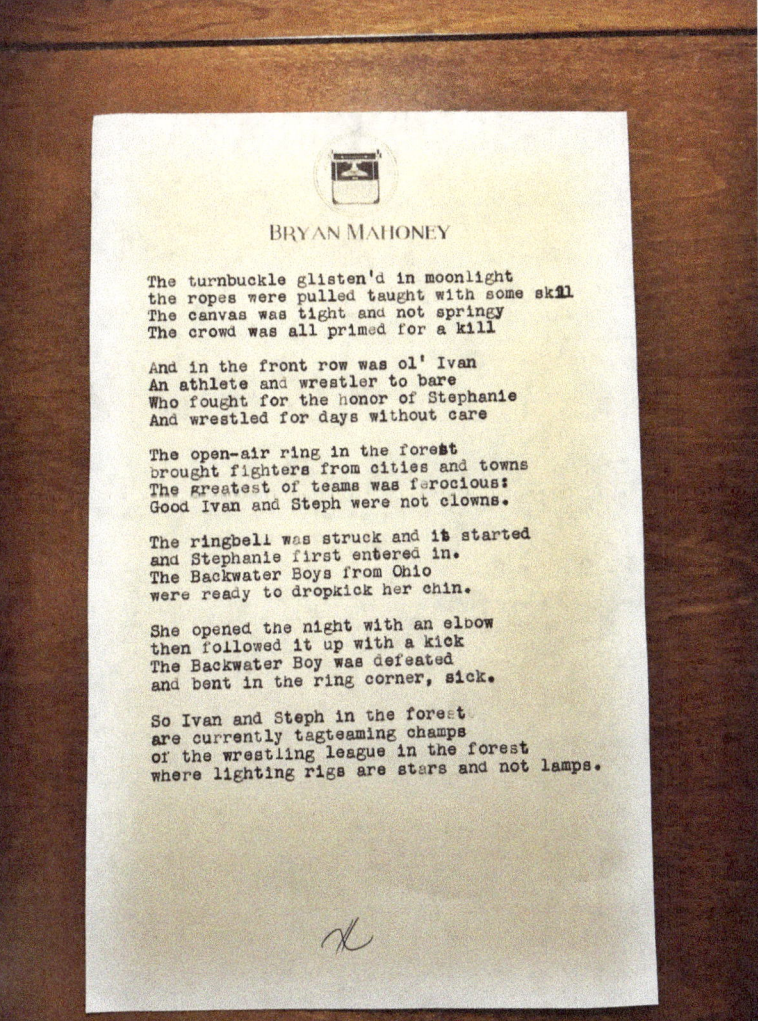

BRYAN MAHONEY

The turnbuckle glisten'd in moonlight
the ropes were pulled taught with some skill
The canvas was tight and not springy
The crowd was all primed for a kill

And in the front row was ol' Ivan
An athlete and wrestler to bare
Who fought for the honor of Stephanie
And wrestled for days without care

The open-air ring in the forest
brought fighters from cities and towns
The greatest of teams was ferocious:
Good Ivan and Steph were not clowns.

The ringbell was struck and it started
and Stephanie first entered in.
The Backwater Boys from Ohio
were ready to dropkick her chin.

She opened the night with an elbow
then followed it up with a kick
The Backwater Boy was defeated
and bent in the ring corner, sick.

So Ivan and Steph in the forest
are currently tagteaming champs
of the wrestling league in the forest
where lighting rigs are stars and not lamps.

the **Typin'Pint**
by Bryan Mahoney

Long ago, a man named Nic
Was born 'neath silver moon
A hero's fate placed on him thus,
His strength, a godly boon

He saved a bus of tourists once
From tipping off a cliff
And lifted up a boulder from
A hiker, lost, named Biff

And every year in winter deep
This hero would arise
The people would bestow him gifts
Cigar smoke fill'd the skies

They sang him praises of his deeds
And offered him a feast
But then one year it was cut short
By uninvited beasts

They tore from deep within the wood
All snarling out for blood
They terrorized the party peeps
Who slipp'd in the deep mud

And hero Nic was in the crowd
Reluctant to get up
For he was partying a lot
And deep within his cup

But Nic let out a mighty roar;
The snarling beasts now bayed
And Nic punched three back to the woods
And party guests were saved!

www.thetypinpint.com

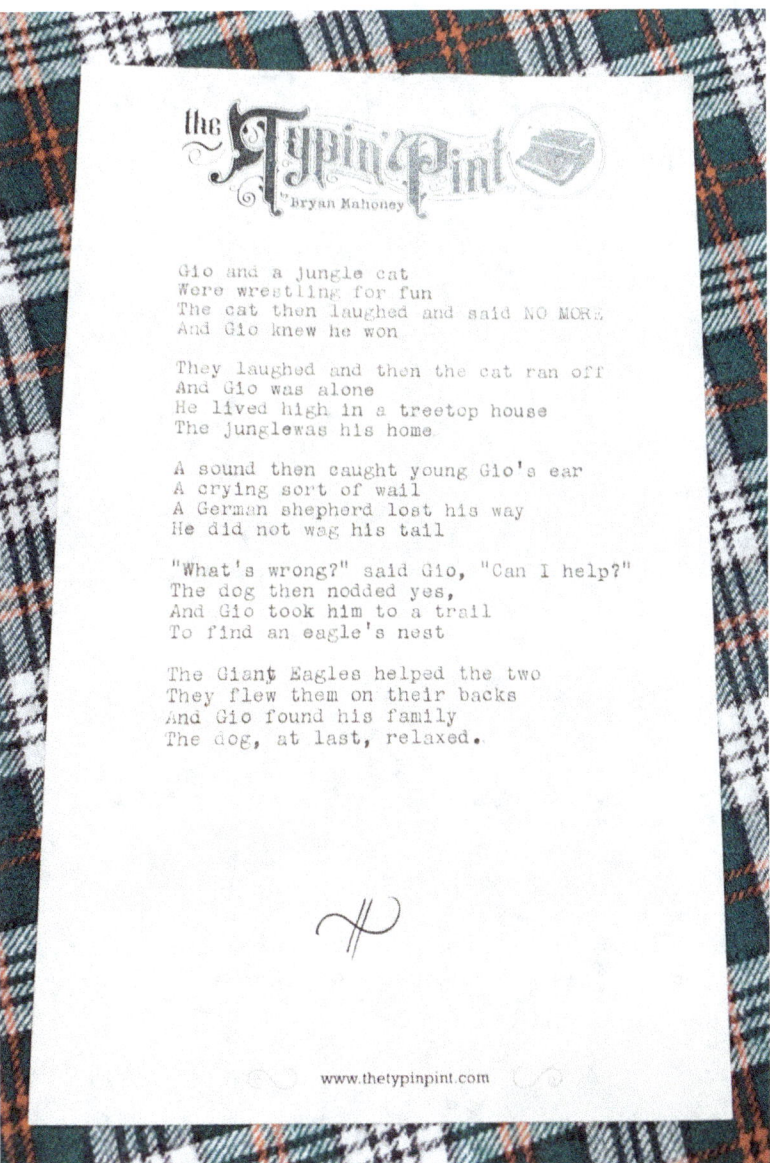

the **Typin' Pint**
"Bryan Mahoney"

Gio and a jungle cat
Were wrestling for fun
The cat then laughed and said NO MORE
And Gio knew he won

They laughed and then the cat ran off
And Gio was alone
He lived high in a treetop house
The junglewas his home

A sound then caught young Gio's ear
A crying sort of wail
A German shepherd lost his way
He did not wag his tail

"What's wrong?" said Gio, "Can I help?"
The dog then nodded yes,
And Gio took him to a trail
To find an eagle's nest

The Giant Eagles helped the two
They flew them on their backs
And Gio found his family
The dog, at last, relaxed.

www.thetypinpint.com

section 1   lost poetry

BRYAN MAHONEY

Dvorah's Day

Deep in a forest of plenty
The healer was plying her trade
Dvorah, the witch of the village
Lived close to where beehives are made

She had a unique sort of magic
It targeted all of your ills
Reliable, true, was Dvorah
When doing her curative skills

The secret, she said, is in knowing
Not all of the sick is in skin
The true centerpoint of the healing
Lies buried in secret within

So all of the folk in the village
Knew witches are where it is at
She's friend to the bees of the forest
(Who help her in ten seconds flat)

They fly and they pollinate freely
These titans of industry work
The village witch helps with the output
(Protection from bears that might lurk)

The sun now sinks slow o'er the village
The healer has bottled the balm
And everyone's eager to greet her
They ask for her help with aplomb

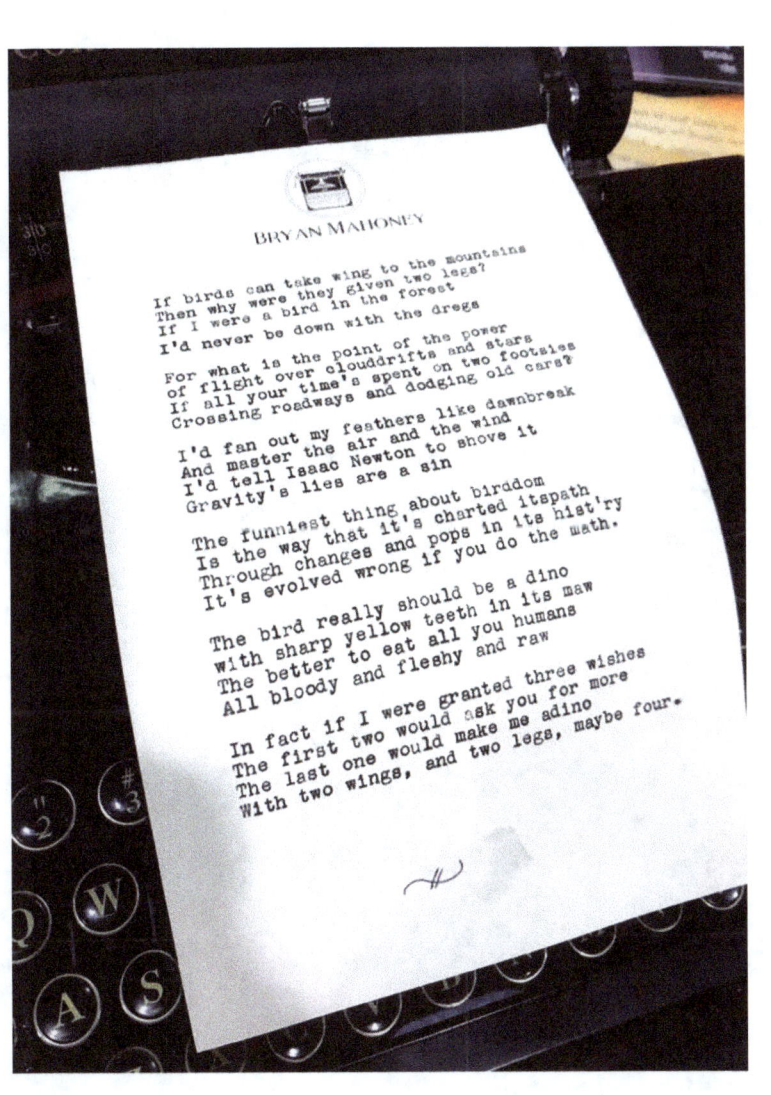

BRYAN MAHONEY

If birds can take wing to the mountains
Then why were they given two legs?
If I were a bird in the forest
I'd never be down with the dregs

For what is the point of the power
of flight over clouddrifts and stars
If all your time's spent on two footsies
Crossing roadways and dodging old cars?

I'd fan out my feathers like dawnbreak
And master the air and the wind
I'd tell Isaac Newton to shove it
Gravity's lies are a sin

The funniest thing about birddom
Is the way that it's charted itspath
Through changes and pops in its hist'ry
It's evolved wrong if you do the math.

The bird really should be a dino
with sharp yellow teeth in its maw
The better to eat all you humans
All bloody and fleshy and raw

In fact if I were granted three wishes
The first two would ask you for more
The last one would make me adino
With two wings, and two legs, maybe four.

BRYAN MAHONEY

There once was a lady named Carol
who drank all the grog in the barrel
She wanted some more
and she kicked out the door
And you get in her way at your peril

the Typin' Pint
by Bryan Mahoney

He's alone at the bar drinking lager
A regular in his own mind
He asks for the sports on the TV
The corner spot's his, you might find

A bubble he's made all aroundhim
And if you make noise in his sphere
He'll ask you to vacate quite promptly
He'd rather have nobody near

In public there's always mixture
The tolerance varies per seat
It makes for a sort of roulette wheel
On what kind of people you meet

So little it should then surprise you
That maybe you're not here for all
And maybe some people want quiet
And put up emotional walls

Some people just want to live lonely
(And that's an observer's cold word)
Perhaps they just want a sound level
That's pleasant whenever it's heard

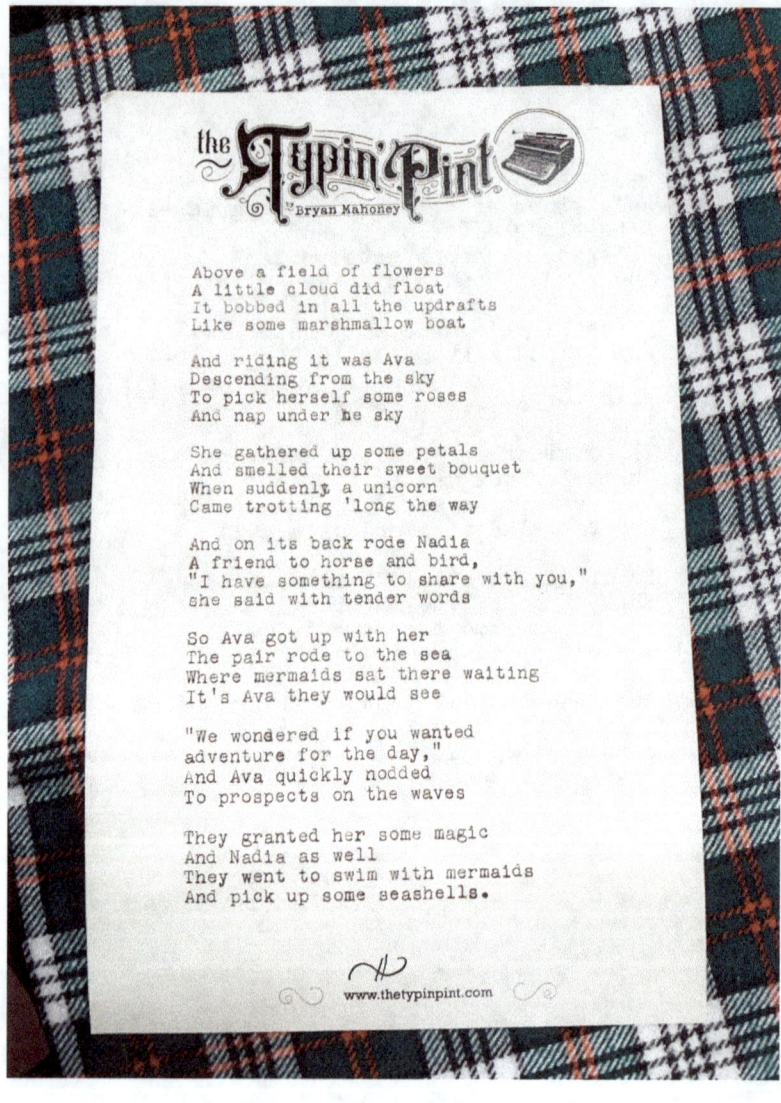

the Typin' Pint
by Bryan Mahoney

Above a field of flowers
A little cloud did float
It bobbed in all the updrafts
Like some marshmallow boat

And riding it was Ava
Descending from the sky
To pick herself some roses
And nap under he sky

She gathered up some petals
And smelled their sweet bouquet
When suddenly a unicorn
Came trotting 'long the way

And on its back rode Nadia
A friend to horse and bird,
"I have something to share with you,"
she said with tender words

So Ava got up with her
The pair rode to the sea
Where mermaids sat there waiting
It's Ava they would see

"We wondered if you wanted
adventure for the day,"
And Ava quickly nodded
To prospects on the waves

They granted her some magic
And Nadia as well
They went to swim with mermaids
And pick up some seashells.

www.thetypinpint.com

section 1   *lost poetry*

BRYAN MAHONEY

A hippogriff likes to go walking
when moonlight appears on the trees
It bows its great head like a sentry
then pushes its wings to the breeze

On cold winter nights in the valley
the hippogriff searches for prey
Anice little beaver is sleeping
it probably should run away

The hippogriff swoops to the shoreline
it drops almost into the lake
The animals hear its wings beating
The hippogriff made a mistake

Now everyone's running for cover
The midnight in form is the fog
The hippogriff botches its landing
and crashes beak first in the bog

BRYAN MAHONEY

Song for Herself

The thoroughfare, wide and inviting,
Brings families and streetfolk and guests
Awoman sets down a black soundbox
And draws forth a mic from her breast

With style she raises the wand up
And slowly she opens her lips
The voice that erupts is a foghorn
That might not invite any ships

The audience speeds up its walking
Avoiding her glassy bright gaze
But to them directly she's talking
And volume she quickly will raise

So ever the tension is mounting
As no one is coming for her
The notes she intones are all piercing
Like claws striking out from deep fur

A homeless man bows down in worship
A welcome divide to his day
He'd normally ask for a hand-out
But music soothes souls, so they say.

And maybe the art of it lives there:
She isn't here singing for you.
She singing for choices and feelings
To feel is the thing that she'll do.

section 2

Love Poems

poems for lovers and poems about things people love

BRYAN MAHONEY

Trip of a Lifetime

In Autumn they started a journey
It started with one little vow
A solemn and heartfelt commitment
That brought them to where they are now

For months now dear Raj said I Love You
And John, smiling wide in reply,
Repeated those words every morning
And often when he caught her eye

They once took a trip 'cross the country
To Michigan, searching a prize
That taught them how they'd be on roadtrips
(A tiny time-chunk in disguise)

The days grew to weeks after wedding
Before long, they'll grow into years
But Raj and her John go on loving
To face life and challenge and fears

A unit they two attack lifetimes
And do so with style and grace
A lovetime spreads wide out before them
To run it is life's greatest race.

The Typin' Pint

BRYAN MAHONEY

Two Hearts

Two hearts were of an era
And distance filled their fate
drawn close upon their meeting
On one specific date

A universe was watching
And guiding them together
It laid out paths before them
Avoiding the worst weather

They say you make your fortune
From hard work and from grit
But in the heart it matters
When you listen to it.

Surrounded, then, by hillsides
The hearts found common peace
With stars above all watching
And plotting, piece by piece

To shrink the depth of cosmos
And distance, culture, time
To bring two hearts together
The stars did thus align.

The Typin' Pint

The Ballad of Greg and Phoebe

The love that our Greg has for Phoebe
Is limitless, grand in its scope
Like seafood buffets on a Tuesday
Or Lever 2000 bar soap

Greg's love is as deep as an ocean
No, better - the Mauritanus Trench
Where light cannot go though it's trying
(It's gotten itself a good drench)

Or maybe his love is like pizza
The dough that can stretch out for miles
The kind that can brighten a household
The kind that brings all sorts of smiles

This love is as constant as phone calls
From pollsters who want your input
But you are just trying to nap here
And you want to match butt with your foot

Yes Phoebe, it's said, is real lucky
In Greg she has all that she needs
For he puts his life in his loving
And that's a real deep thing indeed.

Was it love?

I saw her at the boardwalk
Her hair swept up in wind
I offered her my kerchief;
She glanced my way and grinned

Here eyes became like embers
Her skin a pallid shell
I recognized this woman:
A succubus from Hell!

But in those eyes was longing
That hair, a wispy dream
Those fangs did curve like questions
Her skin like clotted creme

I took her hand and whispered,
"My lady, thou art fair,
And would you care to join me
For treacle en plein air?"

So now we two are married
We live amongst the dead
Was she the one I longed for?
Or was this in my head?

BRYAN MAHONEY

The rainclouds were gath'ring closely
As Amy looked down at the dash
The vehicle's fuel was on Empty
And Amy was fresh out of cash

She pulled to the roadside and waited
The auto club soon would arrive
When suddenly up came a cycle
Its rider: the hottest alive.

He parked next to Amy and gestured
She rolled down the window at last
"Bonjour," said the man, and she smiled,
"It seems that I've run out of gas."

The man then procured her a helmet
He said, "I can give you a lift."
So Amy hopped on and she hugged him
This day was becoming a gift.

They rode 'til the first signs of commerce
A little old shop by the road
With knicknacks & ice cream & flowers
"One of these," Amy said, "He is owed."

They shared a huge sundae with chocolate
"Keanu," he said, "is my name."
And Amy pretends not to notice
His beautiful face and his fame.

The Triple A came with a gallon
Of car-saving gas for her ride
"Deliver it yon," she instructed,
"It's miles away," Amy lied.

She then joined her friend at their table
"All set?" her friend asked with a smile.
"Another poor sap is here stranded,
It seems we're stuck here for awhile."

section 2   love poems

Who they were

The couple met inside a shop
That sold glass jars and baubles
Their interactions first were loose
Like newborn calf that wobbles

It followed soon they spent more time
uncovering their contentness
They forged a bond in common traits
Their soulwork was relentless

They faced the world with boundless strength
Determin'd both to beat it
When challeng'd they held hands and jump'd
And rose as one to meet it

And sometimes when was dropp'd a rope
These two chose else the ladder
To make their way on their own legs
To grow was all that matter'd

But no one can outrun the speed
Of time when it comes calling
So they did more to quench the need
While days and years kept falling

Then out of breath and holding near
They sought a home to live in
Where sunsets followed daily paths
They'd take each day as given

But even in the twilight life
A page a day they wrote
And though they kept their bodies still
They lived in a glass bottom boat.

The Ballad
of Bear
and Bunny

Deep in the Black Forest mountains
There once lived a Bunny and Bear
Their hearts, intertwined under starlight
Caressed by Bavarian air

Adventure became like a trademark
Their company both had enjoyed
Together they knew they would make it
In love, they were not unemploy'd

Together, the world was much smaller
And home was found e'er they roam'd
For Bunny and Bear may be travel'rs
But not ever truly alone

The decades may pass without warning
And age may patina some things
But promises grow without rusting
(ₛEspecially the ones that have rings)

And memories, too, have a lifespan
But keeping them tends to be art
It takes, sometimes, two folks to keep
them
As long as they live in the heart.

So though Bear and Bunny began here
Well deep in Bavarian pine,
It's love that will keep them together
Forever throughout all of time.

"Can you write a poem about Trash Day pleaseandthankyou."

Far past the streetlamps and bushes
My siren-call lumbering near
I take out my sneaks ad my jacket
Then call out, "The Garbage-Man's here!"
He cmes with a truckload of treasure
You smell him for miles around
He picks up your waste in a bucket
And knows when you leave out of town.
For always the trashman is watching
An eye to each driveway and curb
He knows us from that which is wasted
This street sentinel of the 'burb.
The squeak of the brakes signal action
I rush with my baggies in hand
The garbage-man now is a woman!?
The prettiest lass in the land
The garbage-gal said "We should marry"
On Friday he wedding was set
Our families came out for he party
As big as awedding should get
Now Stella and me grab the garbage
On Wednsday we make all the punds
We freely hold hands as we do it,
The loveliest trashfolk around.

BRYAN MAHONEY

Love's where you find it

Sebastian was sitting there, working,
Developing new things to try
And thinking real hard of the workload
(The volume was making him cry)

But then wand'red in fair Alana,
Who had a career on the rise
She told him to chill with the working
(There lived empathy in her eyes)

Sebastian let loose a wide smile
"She's right," thought the man with a grin
"There happens to be more to living
Than jobs that we find ourselves in."

"That's right," said Alana, "And also,"
"The people you're with matter most."
Afeeling then rose up between them
A specter-like welcoming ghost ...

"The first to accede was Sebastian
And quietly reached for her hand,
"There's something I'm meaning to tell you
(These words now, especially grand):

"I think when our hearts do the talking,
It's best to just shut up and hear,"
Alana caught all of his meaning,
And with love in her eyes drew him near.

The Typin' Pint

section 3

Odes

poems about specific topics or people meant to elevate the subject or honor a significant event

Be like the moon

You may look like a round lump

Circling another, more colorful body

A flashier extrovert that people gravitate

But you have your good qualities too, ya know

You are steadfast, and constant, and reliable

You may seem like you are there for only them

But you are your own body, you reflect light

And in dong so you burn so bright

We need people like you too

You help light ways

in darkest

nights

Mimi's World

The world is just art for the viewer
If you have the right eyes to see it
The grasses and trees are the canvas
And if you are Mimi, you live it

Her life she has made into artwork
Her steps in each day are but brushstrokes
And always her spirit creates it
A lifetime of art made in footnotes

For Mimi, a life is worth living
Your heart is the guide of your skill
A day is for making and building
Some hours for strength, soul, and will

In instinct, in sheer force of life,
The strongest get through and survive
The creatures she loves all know something
The meaning of being alive

With paintbrush in hand, she's a master
Of finding the truth in her sight
And with it, her art tells a story
Of living a life that is right.

by Bryan Mahoney

Traipsing through the country
The wand'ring boy is free
To sniff and jump and venture
From here to NYC.

They call him Stitch, the wonder,
And also the best Doggie in the Woggie,
He peeks at you through fluffness
His kisses leave you soggy

If Stitch and you should party
The crowd will flock to him
With just a look he ropes 'em
They'll serve his every whim

He once did live in wint'r
The snowfall, white as he,
Would chill his frame most swiftly
So off he left with glee

Now Cali is his hometown
Where he can rule L.A.
You'll find him there with Lisa
...Adventures every day!

John the Fourth

On Monday, John the Fourth was born
And worlds came into view:
A million time horizons hence
Depend on what he'll do.

He may move men and mountàns with
Commands and fine decrees
He may invent a world in which
He lives across the seas

He may just say some funny shit
(He gets that from his mom)
Or run across the untam'd earth
(Like dad, with more aplomb)

Whatever makes the world of he
It's there for him to take
To march into the vast expanse:
A life of his own make.

A million time horizons hence
Depend on what he'll do.
On Monday, John the Fourth was born
And worlds came into view.

In Buffalo

The hopes and the dreams of a city
are planted in so small a thing
and five dozen men fit within it
for "Bills" the wide chorus doth sing

Identity wrapped in a season
This city owns autumn, it's true
Then out of the ground swells a calling
for "playoffs," then rings we are due

In Buffalo, pride is a birthright
In Buffalo, hist'ry's made
In Buffalo, sport isreligion
In Buffalo, pride is a trade

It's Sunday and church isin session
each fam'ly arrives to take part
The temple is in an old farmfield
where athletes now practice their art

For Buffalo, football is living
A history written so large
It transcends each new generation
Let's circle the wagons, then ... CHARGE!

BRYAN MAHONEY

The Guitar Player

People swerve their hips to avoid him
nearly still, cool tones sliding
out into the open air
Leaning back he's part of the wall
jutting out. They can't avoid the music
He practiced like they said he should,
Craft made for money
They said he'd see it if he stuck with it
He saw the craft
Not the money

An Ode for Ian

What more to be said about Ian?
A warrior bard-dude by trade
Whose skills with a tale fill the legends
of schemings and plans that we've laid?

Can now we all talk of his knowledge
of carpent'ry, history, lore?
Of whisky, geography, Fresno,
Of game rules and magic and more?

Affectionately we call'd them blath'rings
These speeches that Ian employed
And rapt are we all with these stories
For hours most humbly enjoy'd

I have one more thing for young Ian
That hasn't been said - well, not yet -
The happiest fates for your birthday,
We hope it's the luckiest yet!

BRYAN MAHONEY

Bob was a king among menfolk
A regular Renaissance Man
If you have a problem, he'll fix it
(As best as he possibly can)

He wanders around with his trailer
For typers he's out on the prowl
He'll welcome you in with a smile
(So please don't reply with a scowl).

You always can hear oldBob coming
A baritone tinged with the south
He'll tell you a story 'bout Cali
The history drips from his mouth

So ever if you go a-wanderin'
And Riverside crosses your trail
Give Typewriter Muse your attention
Discover your typen Holy Grail!

section 3   odes

BRYAN MAHONEY

Miss Myra was a mermaid
A bracelet rare she wore
Discovered in a shipwreck
Beneath an opal shore

She told her friends "It's magic"
And turned it toward the sun
Its many facets glinted
Impressing everyone

But if I were to tell them
About this jewelry's source
Would they revolt inprotest?
Would they respond with force?

Miss Myra, she was cheated
The bracelet was a con
It started in afact'ry
Not far outside Dijon

The bads were made of plastic
The center is a string
A child once had dropped it
but cried not for the thing

Miss Myra now doth covet
A worthless toy once lost
At least the way she found it
Was lit'rally at no cost.

− Bryan Dy

BRYAN MAHONEY

The Adventures of
Lucky & Oreo

When late grows the hour in Burbank
And lamplights begin their dark task,
There quietly starts a dual sentry
Their markings are their only mask

The first to arrive is one Lucky
A mayor and housecat by day
Then following near is another:
But Oreo knows not the way.

"Psst!" "Hurry!." says Lucky while stalking
And Oreo follows in step
They have lots to fill the agenda
(But as cats, they begin with a *blep*)

Some garbage to dine on could happen
But Lucky knows there's better fare
And Oreo's all about eating
So Lucky will bring him straight there

A restaurant was the night's endpoint
And Oreo soon had his fill
"What's next?" he announced to friend Lucky
"We'll go to wherever you will."

So Oreo pointed east, homeward
"I think now it's time for a rest."
And Lucky, so grateful for comp'ny,
Announced, "Oreo, you're the best."

The Typin' Pint

BRYAN MAHONEY

SuperPumpkin

Pumpkin the Hamster was tiny
But don't you be fooled by his size
For Pumpkin hid well a deep secret
And he often flew through the skies

Its turns out that Pumpkin is super
(and not just because he's so cute)
He comes from a planet of plenty
Where hamsters eat magical fruit

It makes them a fierce sort of fighter
Defeating the bad guys with ease
There's one who can shapeshift to tigers
And one with a powerful sneeze

But Pumpkin got powers of flying
He takes to the air like a shot
Defending the land is our Pumpkin
A hero, believe it or not.

He once stopped a bank heist in Wilkes Barre
The robberst thought they had a plan
But like a fur-bullet was Pumpkin
Who flew in as fast as he can

In seconds he hauled out the money
And pulled it from their U-Haul van
Then gave it all back to the bankers
They thanked him as best as they can

The newspaper wrote all about it
And Pumpkin was on the front page
And that's how we all heard about it
('Cause Pumpkin's asleep in his cage).

A poem, ephem'ral and floppy
Is seldom a permanent thing
Until it is lodged in one's mem'ry
Where echoes of living will sing

Its life may begin here on paper
Before he espresso kicks in
Ideas become ink in the offing
The story is born but it's thin

Then something occurs as it's written
The words form a shape like Jell-o
Then molding themselves into pictures
Ideas to excite or just grow

The poem is bloom'd like a flower
Revealing itself as it grows
The feeling and mood are its power
As long as the muse-song still flows

And how it strikes hearts is the magic
It(s different for those in its crowd
It hits like a dart in its reading
Or music, when spoken aloud.

section 4

Horror

poems to plumb dark thoughts and feelings

House for Sale

Again I feel the tapping -
A finger on my back.
As if to say, "Excuse me,
A body I do lack."

This house is curs'd, I knowit,
Those symbols on the door ...
And what about the staining
Of blood upon my floor?

At night I hear the screaming
A lowly banshee's wail
A death shall come to meet me!
(Which goes beyond the pale.)

And in the barn are voices
Of children who are doomed.
They cut across the acres
Like shards of death untomb'd

So thus you find a listing:
Thishouse is up for sale
It comes with sev'ral roomates
They don't require mail!

There once was a village near Malta
A vibrant and lovely old place
With fishing and farming a-plenty
Festoon'd with great streamers of lace.

And greatest of all were its people
A friendly and generous lot -
They'd give you their beds if requested
Then they would go sleep on a cot.

They'd feed you and clothe you ifneeded,
And destitute all they'd take in
No limits were known to their welcome
To fail this, they felt, was a sin.

Their beauty, it's said, was unrival'd
Their diet and work made them strong
With everything there seeming perfect,
What then, you might ask, could be wrong?

The only strict rule of the village
Was never to go out at night.
For that was the time of the feasting -
The taste of raw flesh, their delight.

There once was a man in the window
A sallow and underfed lot,
Who only appeared in my musings
(and grimaced more often than not)

Resolving in thin apparitions,
His visage lock'd me in his stare,
A milky deep look in his eyeballs
But I'm still unsure if he's there.

At night he's a voice on the moonlight
By morning I hear nought a sound
The moors are alive witha whisper
I wonder if he will be found

My steps are an echo of nothing
The brambles crunch well underfoot
These misty old grounds are an echo
The brambles crunch well underfoot

Returning to home is an effort
A drudging of what I can see
The man is there now in the window
But is he the ghost? Is it me?

Erie's monster

Under the waters ofErie
A creature of Death doth exist
It hunts under cover of darkness
It feeds in the dense morning mist

Its claws are as sharp as a whipcrack
Its scales are of iron and steel
Its teeth will cleave flesh with abandon
Its throat makes a horrible peal

The fisherfolk dare not approach it
Their industry's all but undone
The beast is the queen of the lakebed
Pierc'd not with a speartip or gun

It dines on the skin ofits victims
And cleans off its fangs with their bones
Its mask is a permanent bloodclot
It relishes screaming and groans

I give you this warning to save you
For twenty-five men aren't enough -
The horrible Beast ofLake Erie
Ismade of some nightmarish stuff.

BRYAN MAHONEY

Casting Off

It locked itself in on a Tuesday
A whisper that drove itself deep
A creeping cold dread of a mem'ry
That no one should ever dare keep

It spread to the limbs rather quickly
Insidious sticky malaise
That wrapped itself deep in the conscious
A skin on each thought, breath, and phrase

The thought was a physical nuisance
Lucia could feel her succumb
But she had to get on ~~i~~ with living
And letting it guide her was dumb

She lifted herself from the carpet
And drew on a wellspring of will
That pulsed in her heart ever freely
(Though access took effort and skill)

"But that was the point," she told no one,
"The cure for this dread is in me,
And if I'm to win I'll control it
Andthen, only then, am I free."

Lady Love

I saw her at the boardwalk
Her hair swept up in wind
I offered her my kerchief;
She glanced at me and grinned

Her eyes became like embers,
Her skin a pallid shell
I recognized this woman -
A succubus from Hell!

But in those eyes was longing
That hair, a wispy dream
Those fangs did curve like questions
Her skin like clott'd creme

I took her hand and whispered,
"My lady, thou art fair,
And would you care to join me
For treacle en plein air?"

So now we two are married
We live amongst the dead
Was she the one I searched for?

Or was this in my head?

Meeting the Lady in Grey

The lamps were dimmed down in the study
The wind had a biting bad edge
And Carmen awaited the muses
Who lived on a thin razor's edge

She'd written three chapters already
But Carmen had needed much more
Tonight she would dive into hist'ry
Imaginings would she explore.

Again she called forth the Grey Lady
And fixed a clear sight in her mind
Then, conjuring action, she started
Like justice, her story was blind

The words came out flowing as always
But this time, a whisper began:
"Who calls me from out of my lifetime?
 Who dares to suppose my own plan?"

And Carmen, alarmed, looked around her
For this night, she wrote here alone
Some spirit she conjured in writing
Her voice like a flint scraped on bone

"I'm sorry, I thought you were fiction,"
The author called out to the air.
"Tis I," she replied, "The Grey Lady.
 Now what have you got written there?"

The Bandy Man

The Bandy Man is watching
He waits for you to sleep
Then gives you evil secrets
Too dark and droll to keep

At first you wake in fever
Then when the sweat ahas passed
The Bandy Man takes over
'Til moonlight comes at last

And in your recollection
The day's a misty loss
Your mind's consumed by something
Like roots beset by moss

You lay to rest awhile
The Bandy Man returns
And should you dare oppose him
He marks you with his burns

The morning comes with purpose
You know what you must do
The Bandy Man is watching
The Bandy Man is you.

Fergus Hammertime with Underwood 5.

section 5

Existential

poems exploring our purpose and our place in the universe

the **Typin' Pint**
by Bryan Mahoney

She peered into a pool of light
defiant with its brilliance
Its everglow was warm and bright
Accompanied by silence

She worried if she stared too long
She might incur some blindness
But all she sought was answers and
a little stroke of kindness

For all around her worlds were born
They spun and formed from doubting
She watched them grow from oily seas
Of dissidence and shouting

To tune them out she focused hard
Envisioning a haven
Where things were in alignment and
She ruled them as their maven

The chaos all around her slowed
in universal order
The landscape laid itself in lines
Without a wall or border

And stepping into this new place
She saw it's of her making
Though chnages come and changes go
Her future's for her taking

— Bryan Mahoney

"Ownership is fleeting,"
I heard my father say.
"Be thankful for what's given here,
For it could go away."

That's true of all our earnings;
We can't take them at death
But what about in heaven
Long past our final breath?

Will God permit me clothing
When then my soul's laid bare?
For surely we are rob-d
Ensconced in holy air

To lose something is human;
Regaining is divine
A thing that once was missing
I now reclaim it mine

You might not feel its absence
Or it may drill a hole
If "ownership is fleeting"
I'm glad it's not my soul.

section 5   existential

by Bryan Mahoney

There was a magic forest
Where magic folk lived free
They made homes on the ground here
Or way up in the trees

The gnomes were real hard workers
The centaurs made a mess
The pixies all ate oranges
And wore some sparkly dress

And in the trees lived fairies
They're friendly as a whole
They had a friend named Eleanor
A gentle, curious soul

When Eleanor would visit
The fairies came to play
They'd put on big productions
And parties for the day

Sometimes they made some pastries
For teatime in the wood
Complete with macaroni
(And cheeses, as it should)

But then the day got later
And Eleanor went home
To return there tomorrow
And hang out with the gnomes

section 5   existential

the **Typin' Pint**
by Bryan Mahoney

Crunching underneath my feet
The fallen leaves of autumn
The sunlight gives them golden life
A blessing, warm, upon them

The beams diffuse through ochre boughs
And light the ways ahead
The path is lit and open now
Its hungry ball is fed

I follow something drawing me
It's just outside my view
Compelled to walk this wooded path
It's what I'm meant to do.

This wood holds many mysteries
But so does the unknown
It fills the unlit future and
we all face it alone

But others we can bring along
And join us in our hiking
The wood can bare us better days
The future's ours for striking

the **Typin' Pint**

by Bryan Mahoney

Relationships, like forest paths,
Can take on many shapes
They're often formed by nature
(and sometimes filled with snakes)

But here's the thing about a path:
It's there for you to take it
But if it doesn't lead you true
A path is what you make it

And when you cut the forest off
And leave behind the ages
You start to forge a better way
By taking it in stages

The path now snaking far behind
Had one fair righteous purpose:
To give you all the knowledge now
To forge your way in forests

So even though that path is gone
It lives in some new treeline,
You always can make progress next
For peace, you make a beeline.

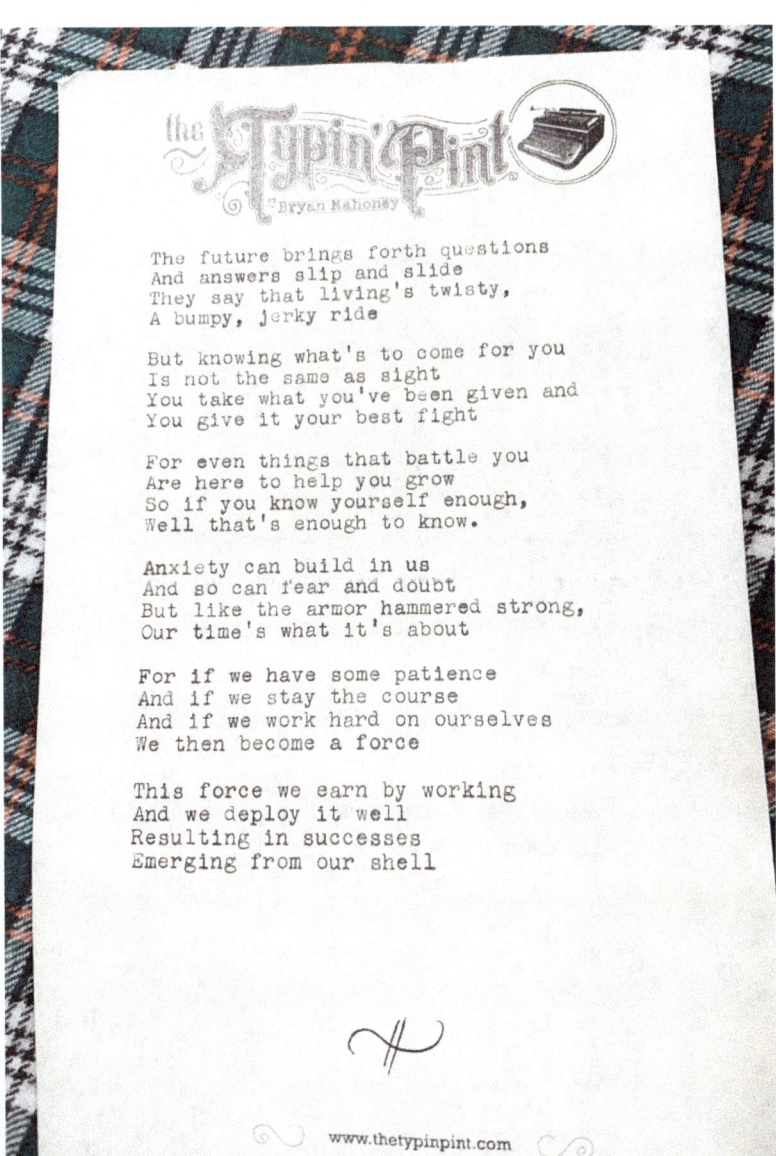

the Typin' Pint

Bryan Mahoney

The future brings forth questions
And answers slip and slide
They say that living's twisty,
A bumpy, jerky ride

But knowing what's to come for you
Is not the same as sight
You take what you've been given and
You give it your best fight

For even things that battle you
Are here to help you grow
So if you know yourself enough,
Well that's enough to know.

Anxiety can build in us
And so can fear and doubt
But like the armor hammered strong,
Our time's what it's about

For if we have some patience
And if we stay the course
And if we work hard on ourselves
We then become a force

This force we earn by working
And we deploy it well
Resulting in successes
Emerging from our shell

section 5   existential

CHASE YOUR DREAMS

Ideas are like dust motes:
The more you try to capture one and
hold it in your hand, the more it spirals
away from you. Try sitting still.
Let it float on its own path, settling
where it needs to. Be the calm
stable surface to hold it.
Then sweep them up and send them
spiraling out into the world.

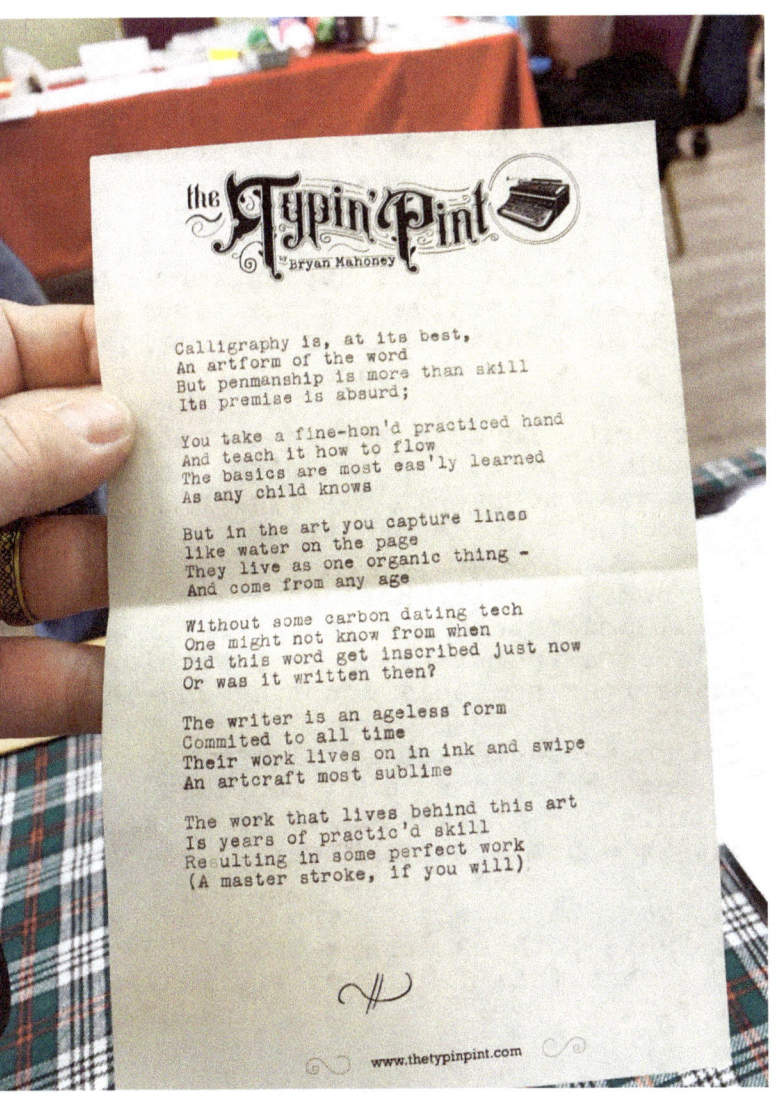

the Typin' Pint
by Bryan Mahoney

Calligraphy is, at its best,
An artform of the word
But penmanship is more than skill
Its premise is absurd;

You take a fine-hon'd practiced hand
And teach it how to flow
The basics are most eas'ly learned
As any child knows

But in the art you capture lines
like water on the page
They live as one organic thing -
And come from any age

Without some carbon dating tech
One might not know from when
Did this word get inscribed just now
Or was it written then?

The writer is an ageless form
Commited to all time
Their work lives on in ink and swipe
An artcraft most sublime

The work that lives behind this art
Is years of practic'd skill
Resulting in some perfect work
(A master stroke, if you will).

www.thetypinpint.com

section 5   existential

Not All That Is Can Be Seen

The universe holds to its myst'ries
Held close under lock and a key
But sometimes the cosmos cracks open
Revealing some things as they be

These moves, as they happen, are subtle
Revealing themselves at odd times
We may not catch them in our notice
They pop up in whispers and rhymes

A pow'rful force comes in secret
It guides us to better bright days
It's easy to say it's a figment
If we don't abide by its ways

Its name is calledHope and it's hidden
We misunderstand how it works
It's born from a place deep within us
Where fear and cold doubting can lurk

The universe inside us plants it
To grow when we need it the most
In this it may seem quite elusive,
But it's not some ethereal ghost.

In fact, there's a powere in hoping
It fuels both explorers and youth
To access this feat look within you
It sits in yourself with the truth.

Luanna's Music

Some music, it's said, is explosive
Some music can make you feel love
Some music will send you ascending
Toward some other planet above

And if you want something bombastic
Luanna's the artist you need
She's got TnT in her bloodstream
And plays violin with all spped

When Lexington heard of her talent
They asked for a concert for all
The teachers from Boston's best schoolings
Demanded the best for a ball

It honored the union of thinking
Two countries were meeting at last
The U.S. envoy to Tobago
Was hoping to throw a big blast

"I got you," Luanna responded
And showed at the ballroom on time
A hush fell among the attendants
To hear violin most sublime

The notes filled the air with her music
And when our Luanna was done
She said, "That'll be fifteen-hundred ...
Do you think I just do this for fun?"

the Typin' Pint
by Bryan Mahoney

In language there lives an old magic
It makes no fair judgement in use
Existence is service to others
No matter how tight or how loose

With words you may choose to exhibit
A surgeon's fair practice in hand
The cutting is felt in receiving
The words, if well chosen, will stand

The universe holds not a weapon
As accurate or as precise
As words when they're wielded as deftly
Or tossed like some hard plastic dice

But in the right mind they're for healing
They've settled all family disputes
Effective as walls at a border
Supportive like metal-toed boots

A lifetime of use brings patina
You go to the ones that you know
It's easier working in shorthand
To let the ideas in them flow

If fear ever creeps in my dreaming
I think of the elders who fade
For them, the words wane and start melting
I want to recall what I've made

section 5   existential

the Typin' Pint
by Bryan Mahoney

The bedroom floor was quite the mess
And covered in some hist'ry
A million photos strewn about
They make a family mystery

A Polaroid showed little girls
All running through a meadow
Another showed an old man's hands
enveloped in a shadow

A family looked out from the square
All beautiful and beaming
Right next to them, a couple's hands
With diamond rings all gleaming

I recognized a few of them
But these weren't all my mem'ry
Events that happened long before
I entered in this fam'ly

And what could these mere snapshots teach
And what might I be learning?
These people are beyond my reach
The clock face arms are churning

I sit among the photos now
Osmosis for the ages
This hist'ry text's a picture book
And I am turning pages

section 5   existential

I see a killer's shadowe
It reaches off the floor
And points me to the kitchen
I amble to the door

The lights are bright and pallid
The metal knives are thin
But following is shadowe
it pushes me all in

A hand wraps 'round the knifegrip
And calmly lifts it free
I wonder who unsheath'd it
The shadowe whispers: "Thee."

the Typin' Pint
by Bryan Mahoney

There seem to be three types of people
That gallantly traverse this world
They're sailing on ships made of promise
And ~~livg~~ sails of true hope are unfurl'd

The first we shall call "An Explorer"
They charge into life without fear
Their energy's spent on discov'ry
Both inward and out, far and near.

The second is known as a hermit
Reflection is what they do best
A measured approach to all living
And love buried deep in their breast

The third is a lover of wisdom
Respect is not given; it's earned
They measure the world that's around them
Then orate with all that they've learned

These sailors are masters of motion
They navigate rollicking seas
But if you are lucky to join them
You'll find youself sailing with ease.

BRYAN MAHONEY

A Night of Memory

The city streets are empty
The only motion: snow
And set beside the ocean
The streetlights amber glow

A single figure wanders
Her footfalls cut a path
The winds kicks up in fury
A winter cloud-king's wrath

She draws her scarf around her
Continues undeterr'd
Alone with thought and feeling
No need of any word

Behind here are long footsteps
Ahead is pristine snow
It's up to her to mar it
A thought then enters: "No."

She can't change where she came from
She's settled where she is
But where she next is heading
Is like some final quiz

Another step is future
The snow will part her way
The skies there now are clearing
They can't always be gray.

section 6

Absurd

poems that shouldn't be written or read but here we both are

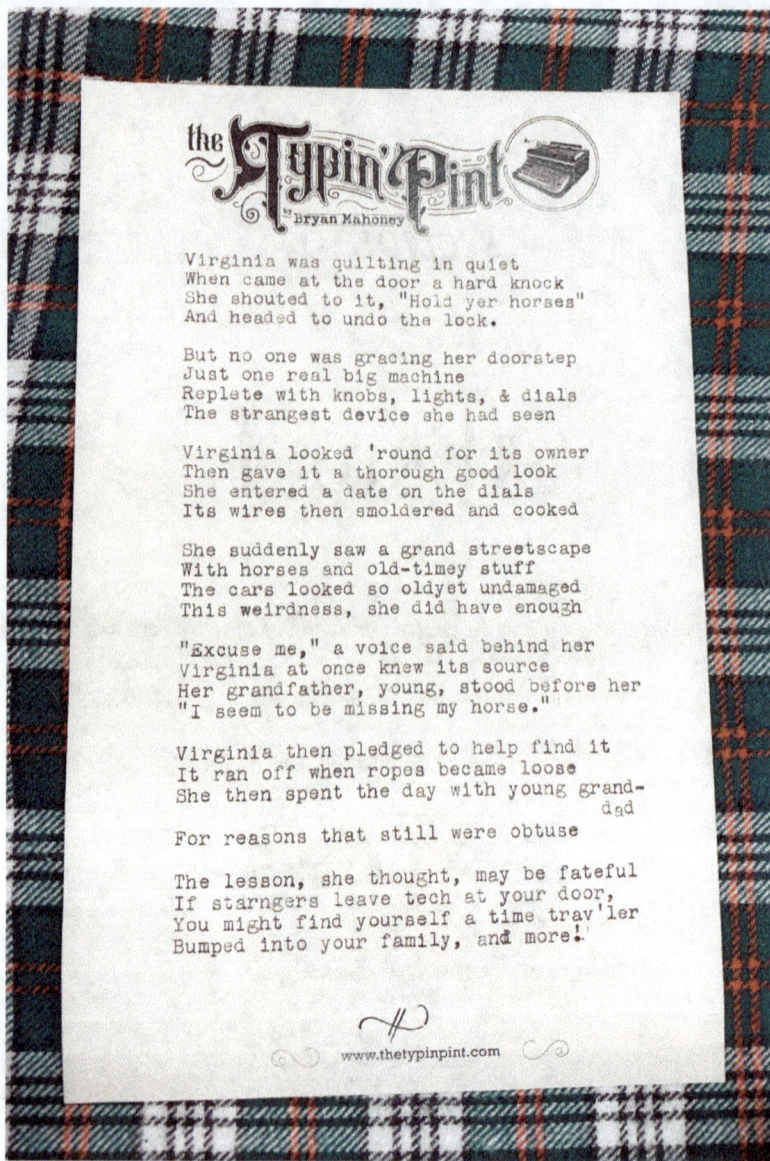

the Typin' Pint

by Bryan Mahoney

Virginia was quilting in quiet
When came at the door a hard knock
She shouted to it, "Hold yer horses"
And headed to undo the lock.

But no one was gracing her doorstep
Just one real big machine
Replete with knobs, lights, & dials
The strangest device she had seen

Virginia looked 'round for its owner
Then gave it a thorough good look
She entered a date on the dials
Its wires then smoldered and cooked

She suddenly saw a grand streetscape
With horses and old-timey stuff
The cars looked so oldyet undamaged
This weirdness, she did have enough

"Excuse me," a voice said behind her
Virginia at once knew its source
Her grandfather, young, stood before her
"I seem to be missing my horse."

Virginia then pledged to help find it
It ran off when ropes became loose
She then spent the day with young grand-
                                    dad
For reasons that still were obtuse

The lesson, she thought, may be fateful
If starngers leave tech at your door,
You might find yourself a time trav'ler
Bumped into your family, and more!'

www.thetypinpint.com

section 6   absurd

by Bryan Mahoney

In Derry where meatpies are plenty
It's hard to be eating just leaves
Despite their nutritional value
They look at you fully aggrieved!

The pies that they make are so lucious
The lard gets a bad rap for sure
And wrapped in embrace is some gravy
And peas and ground beef, butcher-pure!

The piemaker lives in a castle
Of stone and wrought iron it's hewn
At morning it shines like an opal
And looks halfway earthy by noon

She shoves a wood cart to the village
Her wares make a wonderful smell
The street dogs all follow her journey
And where they all go, one can't tell

The pies are the talk of the county
Their fans stretch as far as the sea
The vicar has orders on Sunday
That total one hundred, plus three.

But down in the valley is Willy
He grows and eats spinach all year
He grunts when the piemaker cometh
"You better not bring that 'round here!"

 www.thetypinpint.com

section 6   absurd

"Write a poem about my diarrhea dog."

In winter at its zenith, when twilight skies are gold,
And families in their cabins stoke the hearth to battle a cold
It's best to take to dreaming of greener trees and sand
When floral scents of summer fill your head and sweep the land
This thought had struck young Shirley, who passed the plan along
To Michael, honor'd Michael, who sought to do no wrong
"I've found for us a ticket, to take us from this place,"
He said to his sweet Shirley, a smile on her face,
"So let's away tomorrow. Let's find a corner spot,
An island of our making that makes grace more oft than not."

The plane then left that weekend. Hawaii called them close
They left their home and doggie, who's almost comatose.
"Just look at him—he's sleeping," said Michael with the keys.
Reluctantly went Shirley, who replied with "Tickets, please."
They left the dog with family; a trusted lot were they,
The dog would have his moments filled with food, and love, and play.
The couple spent he weekend in a fog ofwedded bliss,
Returning ona Monday to a home they barely missed.
The dog sat by his dishes, he guarded them to near.
He saw it was his family; he leapt up like a deer.
'Twas Shirley who discovered something wrong with how he hopped
She took a few steps forward and then suddenly she stopped.

"Don't move an inch my Michael," A table lamp was lit.
The dog looked rather guilty on a floor full of his shit.
"He thought we'd gone forever," said Michael through his sleeve.
And both commenced to cleanup of the kind you can't believe.

section 6   absurd

BRYAN MAHONEY

She wanted a rug of the highest degree,
a gentryman's sort of a thing
With daffodil patterns and floral de lis
a covering made for a king

She wentto the merchant on Monday
and dug through the Persians and wools
She reach'd to the back and said "That one"
all cover8d in roosters and bulls.

The scene it depicted was rural
A struggle of poor man and earth
The crops were all dried up and dusty
She wonder'd how much it was worth.

Ten dollars and eighty said Samson
Athird-generation rugg-ier
Whose family had come here from Russia
when farming was done for the year.

She looked at the rug and she wonder'd
if art in the fabric was fused
She then asked old Sam "Are you Joking?"
The merchant did not look amused.

He hefted the rug on the counter
it landed with one heavy thud
The price just went up to twelve thirty
We walked out us two, minus rug.

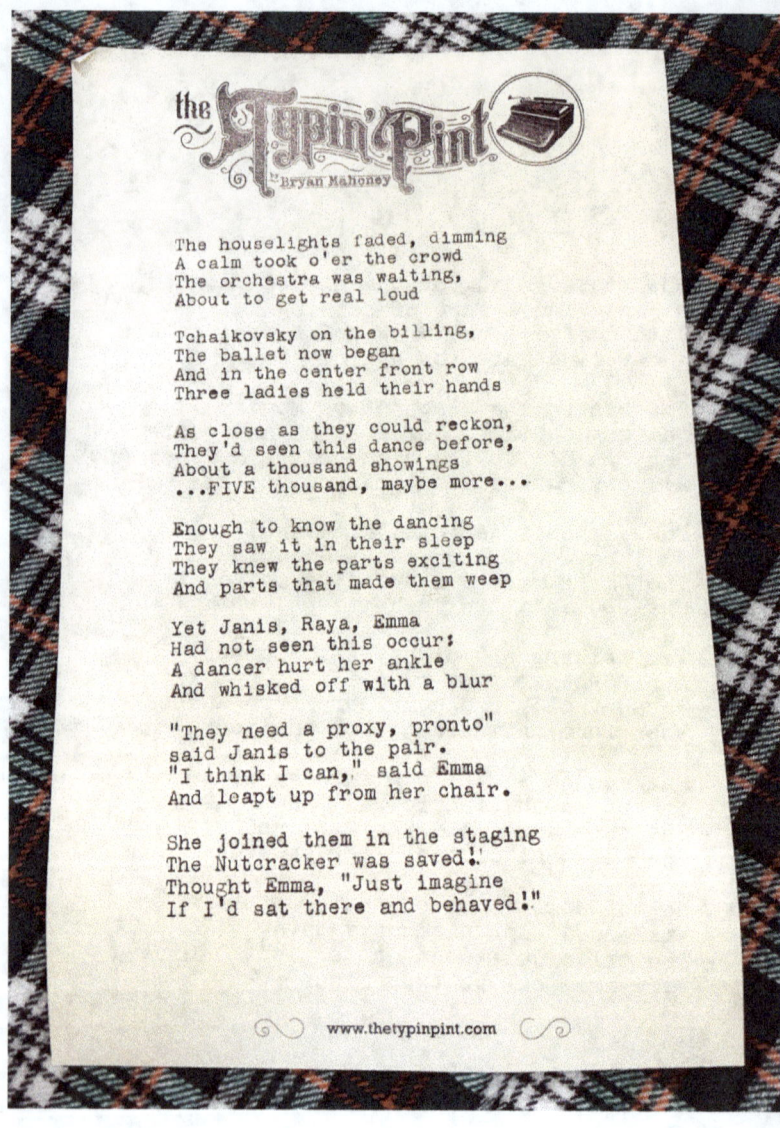

the Typin' Pint
by Bryan Mahoney

The houselights faded, dimming
A calm took o'er the crowd
The orchestra was waiting,
About to get real loud

Tchaikovsky on the billing,
The ballet now began
And in the center front row
Three ladies held their hands

As close as they could reckon,
They'd seen this dance before,
About a thousand showings
...FIVE thousand, maybe more...

Enough to know the dancing
They saw it in their sleep
They knew the parts exciting
And parts that made them weep

Yet Janis, Raya, Emma
Had not seen this occur:
A dancer hurt her ankle
And whisked off with a blur

"They need a proxy, pronto"
said Janis to the pair.
"I think I can," said Emma
And leapt up from her chair.

She joined them in the staging
The Nutcracker was saved!
Thought Emma, "Just imagine
If I'd sat there and behaved!"

www.thetypinpint.com

section 6   absurd

"Write me a poem about Moo Cow Creamers"

The diner next door to my grandma's
Had bottles adorning the booths
They took on the shapes of some heifers
Andspat half-and-half from their tooths

The bottles all said they were creamers
Of "Moo Cow" the model and make
Their primary job was for coffee
To drink from them was a mistake

But that didn't stop us from trying
My sister and I had a race
The first one to drain all the creamer
Would earn them a hallow'd First Place.

We stuck the cow lips in our mouth holes
The liquid fell out with a glug
It ran down our chins and our T-shirts
And oozing like milky white slugs

Upon her return from the bathroom
Our mother grabbed both of the cows
She screamed in a language most foul:
More swears than the diner allows.

We never went back to hat diner
But that didn't keep us from sport
'Cause now we do races at grandma's
With bottles of sherry and port.

Today I am the armadillo

Curl'd unto myself

A lump of skin atop the couch

A soft, conforming shelf

"Write about the Great
Yonkers Cookie Fiasco"

In Yonkers ther once lived a baker
Whose shop intersected two streets
She made crudités
Doused in cinnamon glaze
And the tastiest choclately sweets

In morning the town undertaker
When out for his errands and calls
Would pop in for choux
With a chocolate ragout
And garnished with marzipan balls

The owner once took on a caker
A master of sponges and tarts
She whipped up a batter
(Of what didn't matter)
To show off her custard-filled arts

When armed with a cake-flour shaker
The woamn showed all she was boss
Once all was well mixed
And the oven heat fixed
She gave all the bits a last toss

The bowl had a shoddy Welsh maker
And cracked as the batter was swirl'd
The whole gooey vat
Hit the walls with a splat
And encas'd every place it was hurled

She looked rather grim to the baker
Who tried to give solace in turn
The caker she thanked
But her cookies were tanked
"Without mishaps," she said, "We don't learn."

section 6 absurd

BRYAN MAHONEY

A unicorn's diet is varied
They live off of wishes and dreams
But nightmares will cause indigestion
And a wish ain't as sweet as it seems

The worst things to see in the forest
Are road apples made from their mess
They look just like scoopfuls of ice cream
But taste rather tart, I confess

When you and your love are out walking
and enter a unicorn's glade
Be careful of where you are stepping
Their poops are not seen in the shade

And if you both hear like a whistle
that's followed by several long grunts
That's just a fine unicorn farting
The air escapes fast from their butts.

It smells like your grandmother's baking
Until the one moment it don't
You might want to watch it in progress
But I guarantee that you won't.

The unicorn's face gets all scrunchy
It puckers its lips with aplomb
Then out of its arse comes the farting
like somebody set off a bomb.

"The absurdity of pants. Go."

A tailor once signed for a package
"To Captain" the box was addressed
No name did it bear from the sender
Its cache left the tailor impressed.

Inside were two bolts of a fabric
That ran half his leg as he stood
The tailor then stretchedthem across him
And saw their construction was good.

"A double-pane weave with embossing,"
The tailor exclaimed with respect.
"And look at the cross-frame rethatching -
A method I wouldn't expect!"

The mice in the walls gave approvals
(Just happy for broken ennui)
As they were his only companions
He held the prize for them to see.

"But what with this quarry will happen
Should I put the bolts to the art?
Shall Imake askirt or a jaket
Or a hat to fit old Bonaparte?"

He flipped the sign "Closed" in the window
And pulled out a Singer with force
The shoplights stayedon until morning
And after the dew ran its course.

Pristine was the weave of the clothing
A single long stitch had been sewed
Connecting the bolts at an apex
All sealed up and ready to load.

He first dippeda leg in the portal
Then shruggedon the other with grace
They fit him just so in the bottom
Cinchd tight at the hips with some lace.

He burst out the shop into daylight
(The shopmice all squeaked their applause)
He calledto he world for attention
(His shrieking is what gave them pause)

"I GIVE YOU MY LATEST INVENTION!"
He said without taking a breath,
"I call them my legsleeves of fashion,"
And panting, collapsed to his death.

section 6   absurd

the Typin' Pint
by Bryan Mahoney

The air is one dollop of dreaming
And what now does that really mean?
And why would I write that one sentence
If I were to write out this scene?

Vocabulates come from within me
The words grasping out for a rhyme
And now I lock into the writing
To find a gold word that will rhyme

The verses are bound with the timing
I promise to give a whole verse
But I reflect naught on the writing
When spitting out passages terse

The stories are based on a feeling
It(s easiest making up stuff
It's harder when trying to rhyme them
Then add in a story - it's rough.

But listen to privelege's bawling
I'm lucky anough to be here
And typing some shit for no reason
Delivered by cold-pour'd draft beer.

As long as the paper is flowing
And ink on the ribbon is wet,
It's never too long for the thinking
As good as a side job can get!

section 6   absurd

"Write me a poem about Mexican food"

Marlene made two burritos and left them in the yard
Their marinade was moonlight; she set her dog as guard
"Tomorrow I'll have dinner," she told her hubbie, Bob,
Whose favorite food was mutton, and never held a job
The next day in their driveway when Marlene took off for work
Bob waved her off with smiles which melted into smirks
He leapt back to he table when she drove down the street
To salivate for dinner: The rolled up processed meat
But waiting there to greet him, a toothy hound named Ace
Stood over the burritos with malice in his face
The guard let out a growl, and Bob returned one too,
A staredown for the ages that went 'til half past two
Marlene returned at seven; the house was dark and bare
She called out for her husband who clearly wasn't there
She then checked on her dinner when to her shock and awe
She found her dog and husband - a sight to drop her jaw
They fell asleep together, a plate between the boys
And while they were sleeping she ate the food, sans noise.

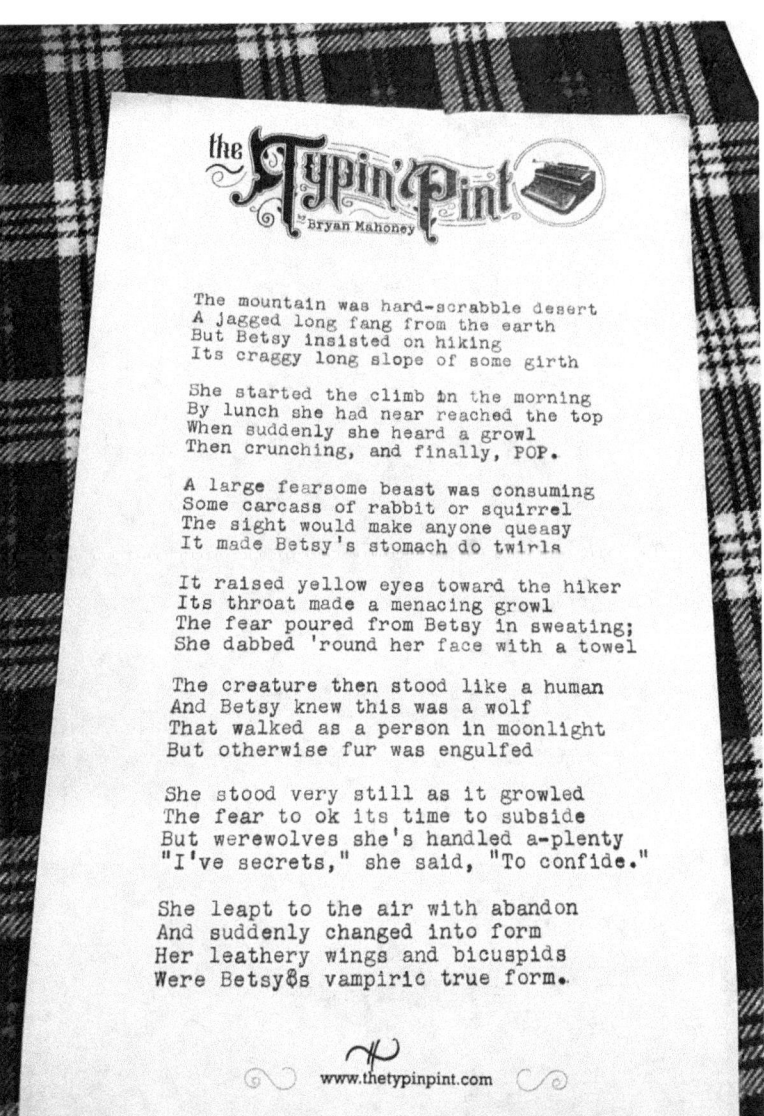

the **Typin' Pint**
Bryan Mahoney

The mountain was hard-scrabble desert
A jagged long fang from the earth
But Betsy insisted on hiking
Its craggy long slope of some girth

She started the climb in the morning
By lunch she had near reached the top
When suddenly she heard a growl
Then crunching, and finally, POP.

A large fearsome beast was consuming
Some carcass of rabbit or squirrel
The sight would make anyone queasy
It made Betsy's stomach do twirls

It raised yellow eyes toward the hiker
Its throat made a menacing growl
The fear poured from Betsy in sweating;
She dabbed 'round her face with a towel

The creature then stood like a human
And Betsy knew this was a wolf
That walked as a person in moonlight
But otherwise fur was engulfed

She stood very still as it growled
The fear to ok its time to subside
But werewolves she's handled a-plenty
"I've secrets," she said, "To confide."

She leapt to the air with abandon
And suddenly changed into form
Her leathery wings and bicuspids
Were Betsy's vampiric true form.

www.thetypinpint.com

section 6   absurd

Bryan Mahoney

A love affair was iron-made:
The Ballad of Chandler & Price
Who bonded close in Cleveland-town
And printing was their vice

They met one night while inking plates
Preparing for a run
Of leaflets for Cleveland's elite
(Plus posters, just for fun)

When Chandler laid the paper flat
His hand brushed Price's wrist
Their eyes locked in, their hearts sped up
The makings of a tryst

And something in their bodies glowed
With white-hot passion's flame
The world fell off outside the two
They forgot, even, their names

So after that one fateful night
The two did never part
United in a love affair
And ink-stained printing art.

section 6   absurd

The Barman's Bitches

The pub opened fresh on a Friday
The patrons lined up for their fill
And Morgan snuck in through the kitchen
To open the taps and the till

The stools were soon stuff'd with the seated
And Morgan conducted his trade
A white foamy pour was his trademark
No better smooth lager was made

As hours sped on so did Morgan
In talking and serving was he
When in walked a cat of the streetside
As cool as a feline might be

But sleeping in back was Ol' Henry
A hound dog as old as the bar
Who slept through all drinking and talking
And snored like a muffl'r-less car

But hearing the cat woke Ol' Henry
He ros with a groan and a snort
And blinking, he sniffed out his quarry
But napping did not oft abort.

Then stretching, he started to chase her
It caught poor man Morgan surprised
The dog and the cat then made bedlam
The bar was destroyed by moonrise.

Rum Punched

'Twas he night before Christmas
And Santa was drunk
Atyrant ofToydom
A playtime-press'd punk

Heswung a he elf folk
He swungat the elf folk
They scattered infear
The soused-up St. Nicholas
Could not hold his beer.

Among them was Midgie
A solid old elf
Who worked out aplenty
(When not on hr shelf)

She stood to cnfront him
Androlled up her sleeves
Then Santa bnt over
And forecfully heav'd

"He ain't worth the effort"
Old Midgie decreed;;
They all left he wrkshop
And did as they they pleased

BRYAN MAHONEY

Out inthe old Emerald Forest
Where Dylan is selling hiswares
He's spinning up 'spresso n lattes
For all ofthe tourists and bears

They come to him late in the morning
Emerging from forest and cave
The little ones run with abandon
And Dylan must say "Please behave."

Then Momma Bear enters the co-op
Her claw-paws and chompers to bare
She orders a honey'd espresso
Before she returns to her lair

So Dylan stands fast at the counter
He looks at the coffees and jars
He wonders how best he can do this
The strangest drink under the stars

So promptly he pours in thecoffee
Then messes around with some foam
The beast is agog and impatient
Her bear feet are tracking in loam

At last he produces the product
A flourish ofhoney at last
Now all ofthe bears come to Dylan
For drinks he can conjure so fast.

"I would like a poem about a luckless leprechaun."

A leprechaun's life is all lucky
Unless you're old Benny MacCool
Whose fashion for gold
Was too easily sold
And you're known as the Leprechaun Fool.

Old Benny tried living in rainbows
And stored all his wealth in a pot
The rainstorms swept through
Washed he coins all ~~atrew~~ astrewn
Benny loses more often than not.

"Write a poem about all those times
we were paid to be reporters and
couldn't believe we had that much
fun at work."

Two writers sat in open air
With life to share between them
To jump and hunt for truetales fair
In moments as they'd seen them

The one did love the stories churn'd
From fate's oft-twisting dial:
The rivers flow'd, the fires burned,
All flung with AP Style.

The other barked a bland decree:
"To government I go
Where law is rule and we are free
And that is all I know."

The lattices of town & state
Twist endlessly entwin'd
If not for they, the Fourth Estate,
Whose common speak defin'd

The oligarchs would settle
Unchecked and free to feast
If not for writers' mettle
They wouldn't feed the beast

It supped and never suffer'd
From pox or boils or blight
Its needs were kindly buffer'd
By cop beats writ at night

The newsroom in its fashion
Would undergo a hush
Then tinny tones of action:
The scanner's morning rush

The soundpricks at the writers
Composing next the news
But somewhere there are fighters
Coached on, and coaxed by, booze

"The cop beat gal will get it"
The writer slyly states
And both go back to Reddit
To read of reprobates.

section 6   absurd

Fish Dream

I woke up with a tingling
It crawl'd way up my leg
I threw the sheet up off of me
It hit my partner, Meg

"What gives?" She yelled so sweetly
Her voice like cherry wine
"My legs! They hurt!" I told her
And fear zipped through my spine

I had another nightmare
The Mob had found my lair
They dragged me from my bedroom
And seared off all my hair

Then tying me to fenceposts
They beat me with a fish
It slapped my skin with fervor
(More violent than I'd wish)

The last attack was shin-ward
And that's when I awoke
To find the fish-bruise redness ...
That dream was not a joke.

BRYAN MAHONEY

A jetpack repairman getsbusy
When all of the roadways are full.
And thiswas the case on a Tuesday
A cold one for tweedcoats and wool.

When Kristen stepped out on the sidewalk
It moved on its own with some speed
It took her 'cross town to the jetshop
To grab her mechanical steed

She shouldered thepack with a shuffle
And flicked on the switch marked IGNITION
It sputtered exhaust from its rockets
Then hoisted itself for her mission

She banked by the Tower of Google
(Named after the old website tech
In ages ago on the web-net
When peoppe used phones to connect)

She flew with her pack to the parkland,
An island that sat in the sky
A relic she took in her pocket
To much the chagrin ofpassersby.

"A book" was the name of the item
And Kristen sat back 'gainst a tree
To lose herself once in a story
What strange aeonspast they must be!

"Write me a poem about narwhals"

I tried to raise a rhino
She lived back in our shed
She ate her weight in veggies
Some hay became her bed

I rode her to a derby
We locked in secondplace
The next heat was in water
You should have seen her face

"A rhino isn't shipshape"
I told her in her shed
Then gave her lots of beetroot
And tucked her in her bed

I entered in the contest
Tomorrow it took place
In farthest North Alaska
Where winds will freeze your face

To ride he ocean derby
You stored your steeds in sheds
So I picked mea narwhal
Between the coral beds

His name was Fickle Jimmy
A grin spead 'cross his face
He bucked and dove and sprinted
And we took home first place!

section 6   absurd

Daniel

Young Daniel had whiskies aplenty
too many for his brain to bear
He grabbed for a glass
And a spirit of class
Now he's silently drunk with a stare.

Young Daniel got up from the barstool
and wobbling, went to the stall
He aimed slightly low
And the yellow stream flowed
To his shoes and the floor and the wall

BRYAN MAHONEY

There once was a troll named Don Pablo
The fiercest old troll in the land
Who pulled people's teeth from their sockets
And tore offtheir limbs with his hands

Don Pablo had muscles and muscles
He lifted a car with his foot
He sat on a boulder in Derry
The rock, with a groan, went kaput.

Along came a wandering sous chef
to tresspass in troll landis bad
For if you run into Don Pablo
He'll squeeze out the blood that you had.

The chef was excited to meet him
For never a troll he did meet.
He marveled at all of his muscles
and all the pink warts on his feet.

Before old Don Pablo could eat him
the sous chef whipped up a quick dish
He offered it up with a flourish
The troll then came up with a wish

"I want you to cook for me always"
He said between bites of the sauce
Spaghetti and meatballs are magic
when you have a troll as a boss.

BRYAN MAHONEY

There once was a troll named Don Pablo
The fiercest old troll in the land
Who pulled people's teeth from their sockets
And tore offtheir limbs with his hands

Don Pablo had muscles and muscles
He lifted a car with his foot
He sat on a boulder in Derry
The rock, with a groan, went kaput.

Along came a wandering sous chef
to tresspass in troll landis bad
For if you run into Don Pablo
He'll squeeze out the blood that you had.

The chef was excited to meet him
For never a troll he did meet.
He marveled at all of his muscles
and all the pink warts on his feet.

Before old Don Pablo could eat him
the sous chef whipped up a quick dish
He offered it up with a flourish
The troll then came up with a wish

"I want you to cook for me always"
He said between bites of the sauce
Spaghetti and meatballs are magic
when you have a troll as a boss.

section 6   absurd

BRYAN MAHONEY

Leap of Faith

The holiday was on the morrow
A party to celebrate life
Where villagefolk came for the party
to leave behind heartach an strife

The tents were set up on the cliff edge
The years gave them rules to obey
The women designed all their banners
The men crafted wood-games to play

Then children, awaiting the starting,
Emerged from the tents to begin
They stared in amazement at all of it
Their spirits all matched by their grins

But waiting is not in their nature
They wanted to start with the feast
The smallest snuck out to the tables
Like little untamable beasts

The first to descend was young Loki
The tart table never had chance
He tipped it clean over in hurrying
And dumped a fruit tart on his pants

Then parents streamed forth from the beer
                                    tent
To snatch up the boy in a run
But Loki had conjured some crow-wings
And leaping from cliff was all done

section 6   absurd

Jungle Ride

There's talk out here in the jungle
Between looming treestalks of glass
That one might, in mom'nts ofwandering,
Lose a mind in the dismal morass

But I, dare I say, found a solvent
That clears all malaise from the mind
It starts with a fresh batch of breathing
Scrubbed clean with the best air you find

You hop on a bike with a motor
You let your loose hair feel the wind
You take all the curves with abandon
And let all the oxygen in

Your thoughts then will find an alignment
An order you may not expect
But careful of truckers and grandmas
Lest all, and yesyou, come a-wrecked

So ending a peril-less journey
You'll find that your life has some room
For hobbies and lovers and study
And time on those things that go zoom.

BRYAN MAHONEY

I ran a good bar in the village
where millworkers came to play cards
Their hands were all dusty
Their thoughts were all lusty
My barmaids were all trained as guards.

The closing bell chimed through the valley
The men would come down from the hill
Their minds would be settled
on testing their mettle
But for every one Jack were three Jills

The worst night on record was recent
As all the newspapers attest
When one man was drunk
and tripped over his trunk
and landed face-first twixt two breasts.

I hired the wench for her wisdom
But she also had muscles to spare
The lady climbed rigging
on schooners in Fidding
and with one arm could lay a man bare.

She tossed him clear over a table
he landed a heap in a snug
When at last he awoke
He thought it a joke
and went back to refilling his jug.

I ran a good bar in the village
on me people always relied
for a good pint of ale
and an almost true tale
and the strongest crew at any tide.

section 7

Personal

poems about specific people, places or events
that strangers and friends have asked for

Bonny's garden

Bonny's garden is wide and strong
Deep roots make good fruit
Tending after it carefully, she puts her
hand to the soil
Feels its warmth, the care of years
Now bears bounty
She shares the garden with he girls
They have gardens, too
Years of tilling, trials, errors
Laughing at the memories

When Bonny gets home she is greeted
by her favorites, all seedlings once,
Tended, guided, grown
In them she sees herself
The hours, days, years counted
not in seconds but in love
There is laughter in the garden
Pattering like raindrops
Settling like dew

Bonny leans back, tired but
satisfied. A life well lived is
a job well done.
There is light in Bonny's garden
Warm, lasting, bright, beautiful light
No time to reflect on it, for there are
seeds that need tending
And Bonny has her gloves on

BRYAN MAHONEY

The Masters of Sport

The seniors were packing the Center
They heard a new sport was in town
And none of them ever tried Volley
They needed a coach to be down

But lucky for them there was Zoe
Who taught them to set spike and serve
The seniors all took to the sporting;
Her lessons were striking a nerve

Except that a serve went akimbo
And now the ball's stuck on the roof
"Fear not," said young Bailey with racket
"I just need a ball and some turf."

Then quickly she taught them all tennis
They set up some chairs as a net
The volleyball though fell between them
And this is a confused as it gets:

They hit the large balls with their rackets
And Zoe and Bailey grinned wide -
They had a new sport, Volley Tennis!
A game they taught seniors with pride.

The Typin' PINT

the Typin' Pint
by Bryan Mahoney

Hannah loves laughing and learning
And Hannah loves numbers and more
But learning and laughing are nothing
Without someone sharing the lore

So Hannah is lucky with this one;
She has a big brother as well
Who helps her with reading and learning
And joining her laughing as well

With letters they're on an adventure
And that's the cool thing about words;
You shuffle and then rearrange them
And they become booms, beasts, and birds

And maybe one day will write Hannah
A great big old book of repute
Or maybe she'll make some discov'ry
Or play in a band on the flute

And that's the best thing about learning:
There's always so much more to know
And Hannah continues her learning
Helped out by her great older bro.

Taking Flight

The sun sank real low on the water
The palm trees swayed slow in the breeze
And somewhere below them, flamingoes
Took flight when a fat old squirrel sneezed

The silhouette filled the pink skyline
As thousands of birds lifted high
Another great wonder of nature
Supplied by a mystery nigh

The scene could have come from a painting
The way all the 'mingoes were framed
And if you were lucky to see it
And cried, well, you wouldn't be blamed

The world was here long before flyers
It spins despite sunsets and sneeze
The world is whatever we make it
For some of us, that's just a breeze

And life in this world is made better
By sunsets and sunrise and sky
The people within it are helpful
(But some more than most, that's no lie)

Like Lindsey, who loves her flamingoes
Who shined like the sparkling wave
Whose smile now powers the sunrise
Whose spirit and love freely gave

Ashley of the trees

The oaks and the elms of the valley
Grow tall and grow straight and grow true
And somewhere beneath an old sycamore
Our Ashley is paying her due

She's captured the magic of nature
A haven enjoy'd in the sun
When walking in fair Pasadena
She met a fae spirit named Glum

Now Glum came from far away shadow
In charge of beginning the night
But when she arrived in the autumn
She thoroughly worshipped the light

"I must have some help" said the fairy
And Ashley was there in a park
So Glum handed over an elm branch
A mission of peace she'd embark

Now Ashley, with branch, is all magic
She spreads the wide joy of this place
And gleefully doing her duty
The patron of nature and grace!

Messages in the wind

The warmth of sun in summer
Brings ease upon the skin
A calm that comes from comfort
And mindfulness within

At least, that's true for Leyla
Who finds herself at last
In walking through a meadow
Carress'd by the tall grass

And lost in thought of mem'ry
She wanders with some ease
Without deadlines to bind her
Just buffeted by breeze

A touch of something finds her
A light caress of wing
Finds Leyla's arm so gently
A multicolored thing

The butterfly is simple
In makeup and design
But patterns there are magic
Like artwork most divine

And soon they number hundreds
And Leyla's not alone
But maybe that's their message:

With us you'll always roam

BRYAN MAHONEY

Joanna's Long hard day

The problem began with the Navy;
A tube full of seamen had parked
In front of the First Bank of Burbank
The place where Joanna embarked

But after a while they left her
Joanna then headed to home
But that's when the dripping had started
A deluge soon rained on her dome

It squirted all over the streetscape
In puddles, congealing at will
It took lots of skill to avoid them
Except for the one deeply filled

Joanna had slipped in the water
And sank nearly flush to her thigh
Obscenities flew from her promptly
And ended with, "Why God, oh why?"

But finally she made it home safe
Or safely as bad luck would bear
Joanna's hard day might be over
It's long, hard and throbbing out there.

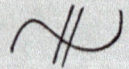

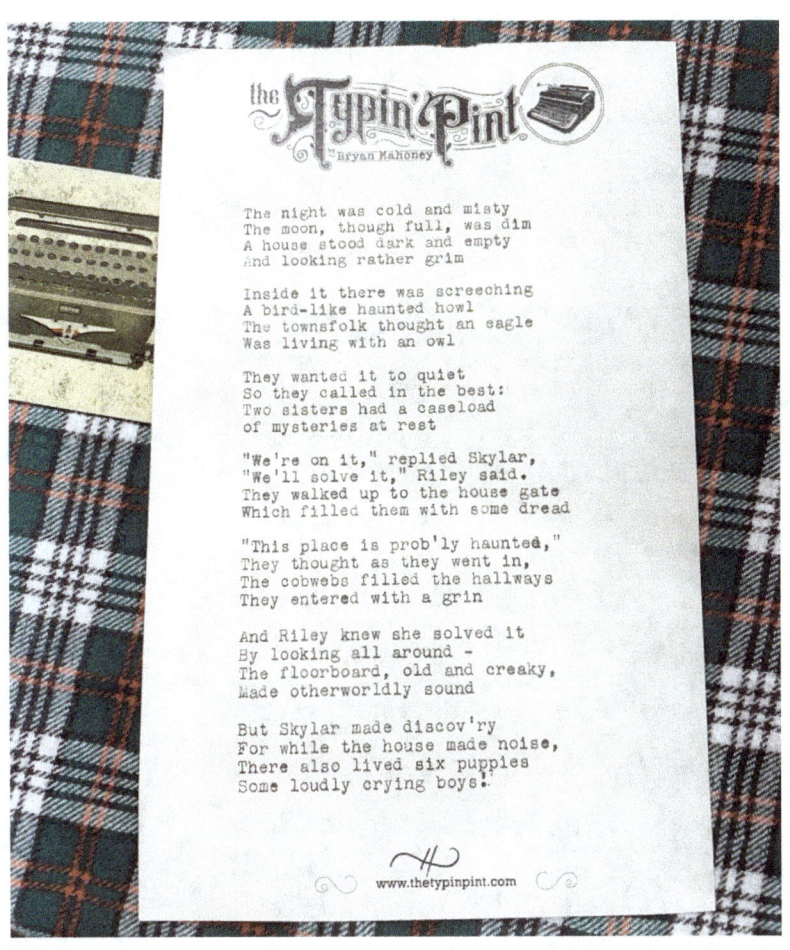

the **Typin' Pint**
by Bryan Mahoney

The night was cold and misty
The moon, though full, was dim
A house stood dark and empty
And looking rather grim

Inside it there was screeching
A bird-like haunted howl
The townsfolk thought an eagle
Was living with an owl

They wanted it to quiet
So they called in the best:
Two sisters had a caseload
of mysteries at rest

"We're on it," replied Skylar,
"We'll solve it," Riley said.
They walked up to the house gate
Which filled them with some dread

"This place is prob'ly haunted,"
They thought as they went in,
The cobwebs filled the hallways
They entered with a grin

And Riley knew she solved it
By looking all around -
The floorboard, old and creaky,
Made otherworldly sound

But Skylar made discov'ry
For while the house made noise,
There also lived six puppies
Some loudly crying boys!

www.thetypinpint.com

the Typin' Pint
by Bryan Mahoney

The universe, vast, cold and empty
Is only this way in our minds
There's actually billions of touchpoints
They're just sometimes tricky to find

The space between stars isn't empty
It's filled with the things we can't see
The same can be said between people;
We're all out here trying to be.

And if we forge some new connection
A chance meeting, disparate souls
The universe puts us together
No matter our wishes or goals

Take Don, as example, a father
Nebraska his roots, corn his trade
He's speeding along in his Mustang
The master of friendships he's made

Relationships ever worth keeping
Are not like some dark hole in space
They're real, flesh and bone, and they're
                                    living
They occupy physical space.

They grow to the outside from feeling
Their source is a forge in the heart
They take form in faces of children
A father like Don's greatest art.

Nia the Bold

On Wednesday was born a fierce lady
Miss Nia came into the world
Announcing herself like a comet
A streak of hot energy whirl'd

She flew into life with abandon
And suddenly, something was clear
A lifetime's potential was packaged
In one tiny unit held near

In Nia there lives the potential
to solve the great ills of our age
She might invent starships or artwork
Or world-changeing poetry page

Whatever she does will be epic
A wondorous life Nia lives
She'll laugh and she'll cry with successes
Her love is as much as she gives

A fireball born was our Nia
A fireball she'll ever be
With love and support from her family
Grown strong as the mightiest tree

the **Typin' Pint**
by Bryan Mahoney

Lelaina was an artist
Her talent was reknown
She traveled through the landscape
Though rarely was alone

When drawing, people sought her
To watch the pro at work
They huddled 'round her drawing
(and some stood back and lurked)

One day when in Manhattan
Leilana drew a land
A magic forest teeming
with fairies from her hand

Then one of them was waving
They asked her to come in
Leilana's art was magic
A place she'd never been!

Her drawings now are famous
There's one up in The Louvre
And if she wants to visit
Her pen gets in the groove!

For Johanna

In life, you won't meet many
who have Johanna's flair
or thoughtfulness or friendship
(in case you're unaware)

She's driven in her writing
creative to her core
her colleagues all adore her
(she's left them wanting more)

Adventures now beseech her
and challenges await
Johanna's primed to face them
at Pasadena's gate.

But first, some words of wisdom:
from friends in far Pawnee:
"Just tret yo'self, Johanna,"
"Fierce power" says Leslie.

A change is just a process,
it's not some grand to-do;
Some caring friends will help it;
they care, a lot, for you.

BRYAN MAHONEY

Always the Supermom

Gracious, supportive and giving:
Three words that tell part of a tale
For Lori is more than some phrases
(Her actions speak words without fail)

There walk on this Earth certain people
Who give without asking for pay
Who honor their families with action
(But also in all that they say)

"You hungry?" means I'm here to feed you
"You tired" means let me give rest
"You sure?" Means I want all the best things
When life gives you relenless tests

And that's what we think of with Lori
A long-suff'ring Mom who is great
Who centers herself in her fam'ly
And guides them to prosperous fate

A day ain't enough for our Mothers
A page can't write down all their worth
For Lori, her son is just thankful
For all that she's done since his birth.

The Typin' Pint

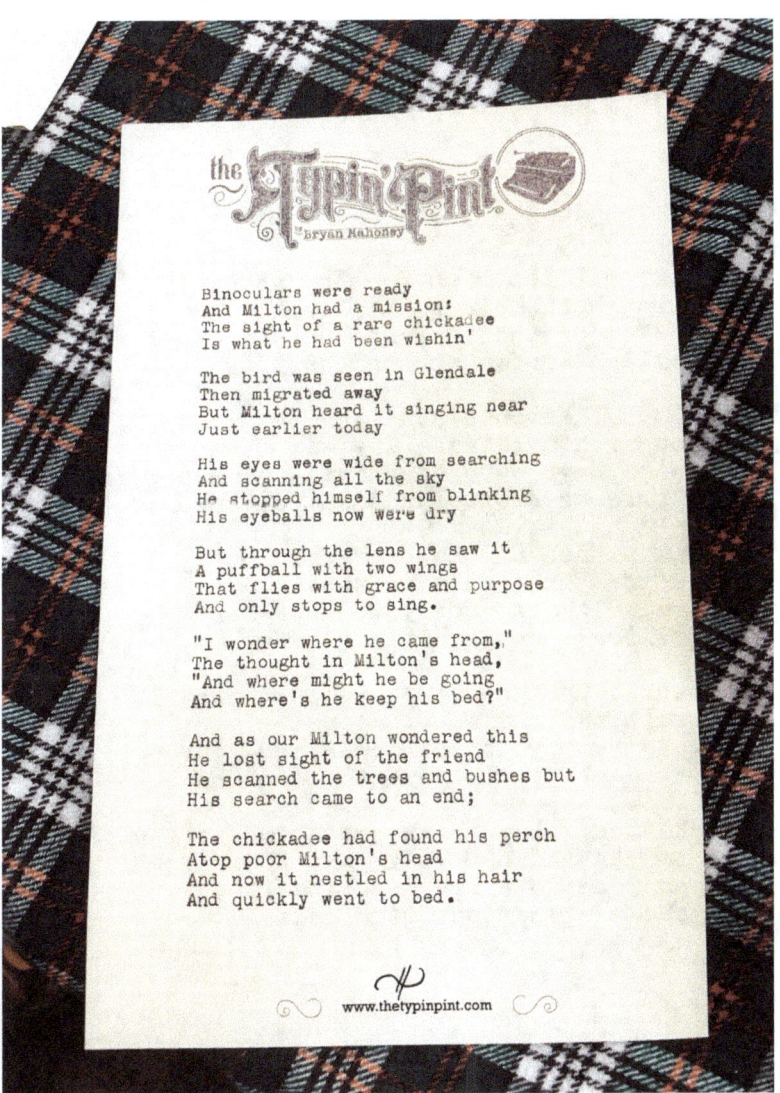

the Typin' Pint
by bryan mahoney

Binoculars were ready
And Milton had a mission:
The sight of a rare chickadee
Is what he had been wishin'

The bird was seen in Glendale
Then migrated away
But Milton heard it singing near
Just earlier today

His eyes were wide from searching
And scanning all the sky
He stopped himself from blinking
His eyeballs now were dry

But through the lens he saw it
A puffball with two wings
That flies with grace and purpose
And only stops to sing.

"I wonder where he came from,"
The thought in Milton's head,
"And where might he be going
And where's he keep his bed?"

And as our Milton wondered this
He lost sight of the friend
He scanned the trees and bushes but
His search came to an end;

The chickadee had found his perch
Atop poor Milton's head
And now it nestled in his hair
And quickly went to bed.

www.thetypinpint.com

section 7   personal

Super Keaton

The bar was set high for the student
Devoting her brain to her work
Here eyes on the screens and the pages
In daylight and when shadows lurk

At times, Keaton's studies were grueling
And other times, case law was clear
And some days were spent without show'ring
(Her friends all refused to come near)

In times such as these we are lonely
Alone in a steep, heavy task
It feels like a steady long pressing
If smiling's on us, it's a mask

But this, it turns out, is just mental
In truth, we are never alone
There's family, and friends, and our neighbors
Who send all their love far from home

For Keaton, they think she's impressive
Her smarts and her work make them proud
A poem from Cath may describe it
But she also screams it aloud!

"I just need something on mermaids"

Far in the deepest of oceans
Two mermaids ruled over he seas
Victoria owned her own nightclub
And Jessica did as he pleased.

The Oyster Bar had all the sturgeons
Victoria served them their drinks
But bars underwater are tricky
Because they're essentially sinks

Then one day this guy with large mussels
come wandering in from the reef
With Jessica working as bouncer
She asks for ID from the creep

"You don't know King Triton?" he asks her
And Jessica gives him a stare
"Without an ID you are no one
And you certainly don't get in there."

Victoria sees the commotion
But she's not so kelpless, you know
She wipes the sandbar and approaches
A bouquet of flounders in tow

"No ID, no service," she tells him.
The king looks all sour and such
The mermaids then grab him and toss him
The Oyster Bar has no free lunch.

Jackie and Thom in Slumberland

The TV was blaring in rainbows
A colorful mix of cartoons
And Jackie and Thom lay there sleeping
(They'd been hard at work before noon).
When suddenly there was ashaking
"Get up," Jackie cried, "It's a quake!"
The bed then arose to the window
No glass or panework did it break
Instead they flew out to a forest
Great trunks yielded pine boughs and cones
"We're not in L.A.," Thom said, whisp'ring,
The forest air chilling his bones.
"Mrow wow," said a voice from the bedsheets
For Roxy and Chaud now appear'd
They'd snuggled at first for some sleeping
But now, foating up, were afeared
Aspaceship then hovered above them
"NO WAY," Jackie said, "Let's get movin'."
A column oflight then engulfed them
She leaned to he right to elude them.
They flew over castles and valleys
The stars high above were heir guide
They set themselves down in Hawaii
And caught several breaths from the ride
Now stranded, the pair took to walking
With Roxy and Chaud close behind
And shortly an arcade appear'd there -
Atruly miraculous find!.
They caught the first flight back to Burbank
And wonder'd about the strange night
And Googled new bedframes and sheet sets
It took the whole oceanwide flight.

BRYAN MAHONEY

Jamila and the Magic Stone

While walking on a weekend,
Jamila found a park
It wasn't there last weekend
They built it after dark

She wandered in to see it
And sat upon a swing
And back and forth she rode it
Then saw a shiny thing

A rainbow stone embedded
and half-stuck in t he dirt
She took it home to Luis
But cleaned it with her skirt

It shined and sparkled freely
Luis said, "Give it here!"
Then took it to Arturo
Who l nt them both his ear,

"It's mine," Jamila stated,
"Now share," came Rocio's voice,
The stone then in that moment
Gave everyone a choice:

"I'll grant you all three wishes,"
The stone said in low tones
"I am a voice for wanting,
Just one of many stones."

So now they all are wishing
for boats and cars and cash
But their one greatest tresure
is a family that lasts.

BRYAN MAHONEY

CASEY THE ARTIST

THE GALLERY OPENED
AROUND EIGHT O'CLOCK
THE PATRONS ALL WAITING
IN LINE 'ROUND THE BLOCK

YOUNG CASEY THE ARTIST
HER WORK ON DISPLAY
HER PAINTINGS OF FORESTS
THE FOCUS TODAY

SHE PAINTED SOM PALM TREES
AND CACTUS AND PINES
THE PAINTINGS FILLED WALLSPACE
WITH BRANCHES AND VINES

BUT ARTWORK IS MAGIC
FOR CASEY IT'S TRUE
HER PAINTINGS ARE PORTALS
TO PLACES ANEW

SO THAT'S WHY THE CITY
HAS COME HERE TONIGHT
TO SEE ALL HER PLANTLIFE
AND SEE DREAMS TAKE FLIGHT

The Potter & The Plant Lady

There once was apotter of plenty
Dear Gladys could mold with some skill
She bent the warm clay into objects
That flowedwith some movement, yet still

One day while out in her workshop
Our Gladys completed apot
A shapely nice form of a woman
Who promptly declared, "I am HOT!"

But Gladys looked 'roundin her workspace
"Who said that?" she yelled to he air
The pottery said, "Well, you made me
My voice is just yours, to be fair."

AndGladys stared down in amazement
For never did artwork dare speak
And this was just one of a series:
The seventh such vesel this week!

But none of them ever had knowledge
Surprise - now the art's elf aware.
And judging by Pot's first assessment,
Is happy with how Gladys fared.

Now galleries 'round seek her potting
And Gladys is very well known -
The Potter of Breasts is her handle
Which Gladys admits with a groan.

BRYAN MAHONEY

Emma's Adventure

The evening was perfect for reading;
The wind battered window and door,
And Emma had found a new story
On sale for two dollars and four!

The title was what most intrigued her:
"The tale of the unfinished life"
A story of action and intrigue
The spine had a shield with a knife

She opened the book to inscriptions:
"To Emma, who says she loves plot,"
Then suddenly, light did engulf her
You'd think this was fun but it's not

She spun and she flipped in a vacuum
Then stumbling, fell on some earth
And found herself out in a jungle
Facing gorillas of girth

She hopped up and spun from the beasties
Then running, she sped through the trees
And hurdled a creek without thinking
And tripped on a log full of bees!

And that's when she found she was holding
The hardcover book from the store
She closed it, and woke in her bedroom
And smiling, cracked open once more ...

The Typin' Pint

Marimba Magic

Cacophony's not quite the word
To properly convey
The bedlam just outside the pit
When "The Last Lap" is played

The battery just does its thing
The drumline all a clatter
But they can't cope without the pit:
Marimba's all that matter

And on the instrument is Eve
She's banging out the tune
The rhythm fills her wrists and arms
The melody goes BOOM

No junior high is better than
When Eve plays with her friends
Excitement fills the stadium now
The crowd hopes there's no end

The music swells toward its finish
And Eve delivers the juice
Marimbas make the crowd go wild
And shake their bodies loose!

the **Typin' Pint**
by Bryan Mahoney

Camila's Best Summer

The last day of school was a frenzy
Camila was first to run out
Her friends followed closely behind her
'Cuz that's what a friendship's about

They first hit the beach on a Friday
Some shaved ice and soft drinks were had
Then they found a farm of alpacas
(@lpaca-back races are rad).

The next week they went to the movies
A premiere of blockbuster rank
But music therin was lackluster,
The singing group's pianist stank.

"I might do them better," said Charli.
"I bet," was Camila's reply.
"Let's try it," Giselle said forthrightly.

"Oh no," then said Jasper. "Now? Why?"

They took to the stage and they nailed it.
An agent took note and said "Wow-
"I'll put you on tour," she said, quickly
"OK," said Camila, "But how?"

The next couple weeks wwre real blurry
Camila and friends went on tour
They made all the money and then some -
For beach days and shaved ice galore!

section 7   personal

BRYAN MAHONEY

The Magic Typer

The art store had only just open'd
Mysterious crafts lie within
And maybe there's something for drawing
Thought young Angelina with grin

A pile of paper called to her
It felt soft and cool to the touch
She looked all around for the pricetag
A dime? Just a dime? That's not much!

She took a sheet home for the weekend
And sang all the way to her room
A canvas for me, Angelina!
A bright spot to cut through the gloom

She rummaged around for a pencil
A black magic marker she found
And concentrating on the art craft
Looked up for a subject around

She started some lines for a figure
Who jumped off the page mighty fast
This magic art paper gave life here
For drawing, it's not Angie's last.

The Typin' Pint

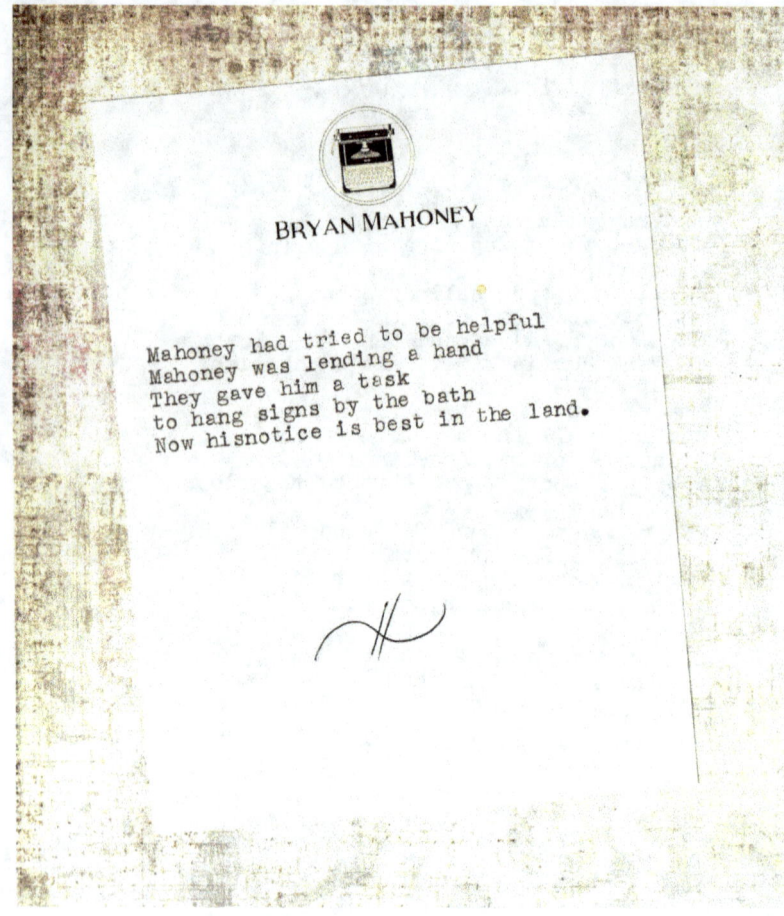

BRYAN MAHONEY

Mahoney had tried to be helpful
Mahoney was lending a hand
They gave him a task
to hang signs by the bath
Now hisnotice is best in the land.

the Typin' Pint
by Bryan Mahoney

Tonight the wind is whipping
It's brushin' in the cold
In search of warmth is Buddy
(As always, truth be told).

But Mark right now is busy
So Buddy wants his lap
And when Mark gives refusal
He settles for a nap

Mark's sitting at his keyboard
A story issues forth
A history of people
From some land in the north

It's like he's living with them
So rich are his bold words
He sees the fiction's landscape
The rivers, beasts, and birds

The sky then opens 'round him
He's sitting in a field
And only Buddy's joined him
(The tuft'd grass appeal'd)

They sat in steady silence
Until Mark's words were done
They both transported homeward
And Mark said, "That was fun."

Stacy's Treasure

Early on a Sunday
When harsh felt the Spring sun
Stacy did some hunting
For free stuff just for fun

She met up with a wizard
Ofering some spells
And giving out some pillows
That squished down rather well

She hunted for some treasure
Or things she might not need
But things that find new uses
Are useful things indeed

So Stacy grabbed some spellbooks
The best the wizard wrote
And flipping through their contents
Our Stacy found a note:

"To someone who is wanting,
Or someone who has plenty,
These gifts are yours for taking
Amass'd since Twenty-Twenty."

BRYAN MAHONEY

Pedal to the Metal ...
er, Alt Rock.

The Hollywood Bowl was electric
The crowd seethed and screamed with delight
The opening acts were all over
The main event taking the night

When Jawbox arrived they erupted
The band looked all suited for fun
But several chords in came a problem
The music came quickly undone

But in the third row, Scott was ready
He saw the problem right away
The wrinkle, he saw, was the pedal
Its hookup was worn out and frayed

"I've got it!" cried Skot with abandon
And sprinting, rushed up to the stage
He dove for the pedal in question
Security staring with rage

Then suddenly, sound filled the speakers
And Jawbox was ready to play!
And suddenly, Scott was then lifted
"A set?" asked Kim C., "Whaddya say?"

The Typin' Pint

section 7 personal

BRYAN MAHONEY

From Mountain to Marketown

Beneath the stepp'd Great Mountains
Two girls camped by a pine
They rode there in a shoebox
A car of grand design.

They came there from old Marketown
A bustling zoo of a place
Ruled sagely by King Brownie Dog
With poise, and charm, and grace.

They traveled through Elm Valley
A place of molded clay
Where love had powered golems
And fueled the sisters' play

A house of cards was built there
It sprawled across the land.
The girls became its architects;
'Twas built by steady hands.

The hour's late for camping
Adventure comes with dawn
"Goodnight" they say to their kingdoms
Their fantasy's light remains on.

The Typin' PINT

the Typin' Pint
by Bryan Mahoney

Now Gary, once, in Germany
Ate schnitzel by the pound
Assistant to the chaplain
(And the best, I'm told, around)

A dairy farm he hails from
The Midwest was his land
The man from Minnesota
Was sax-y in the band

In high school he was president
The top among his peers
Then college showed him medicine
He'd crack backs through the years

His superpower, many:
In parking he's the best
His id is primal instinct
In naps he doth invest

But in all Gary's feats and deeds
He's propped up by his girls;
For joining him is Geraldine
in road trips in the world

And Kim and Christy also add
some spice into his days
He ain't some Lonesome Fugitive
He's loved in many ways!

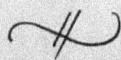

BRYAN MAHONEY

The stagelights were bursting with fire
And Cortney was ready to play
Her vocal chords washed with some lemon
The crowd was a good one today

They had no idea what was coming
As Cortney had started to sing
The tune was a slipp'ry old standard
But myst'ry was off in the wings

As Cortney approached the refraining
A curtain was thrown far and wide
A wild attacker named Becky
Emerged with a knife at her side

She swept by the stage with abandon
And raising the blade did descend
On Cortney, completing an A chord
Did not know that this was her end.

The blood turned the ivories a crimson
The audience screamed and got out
And Cortney, now covered in ketchup,
Hugged Becky, accomplice no doubt.

THE TYPIN' PINT

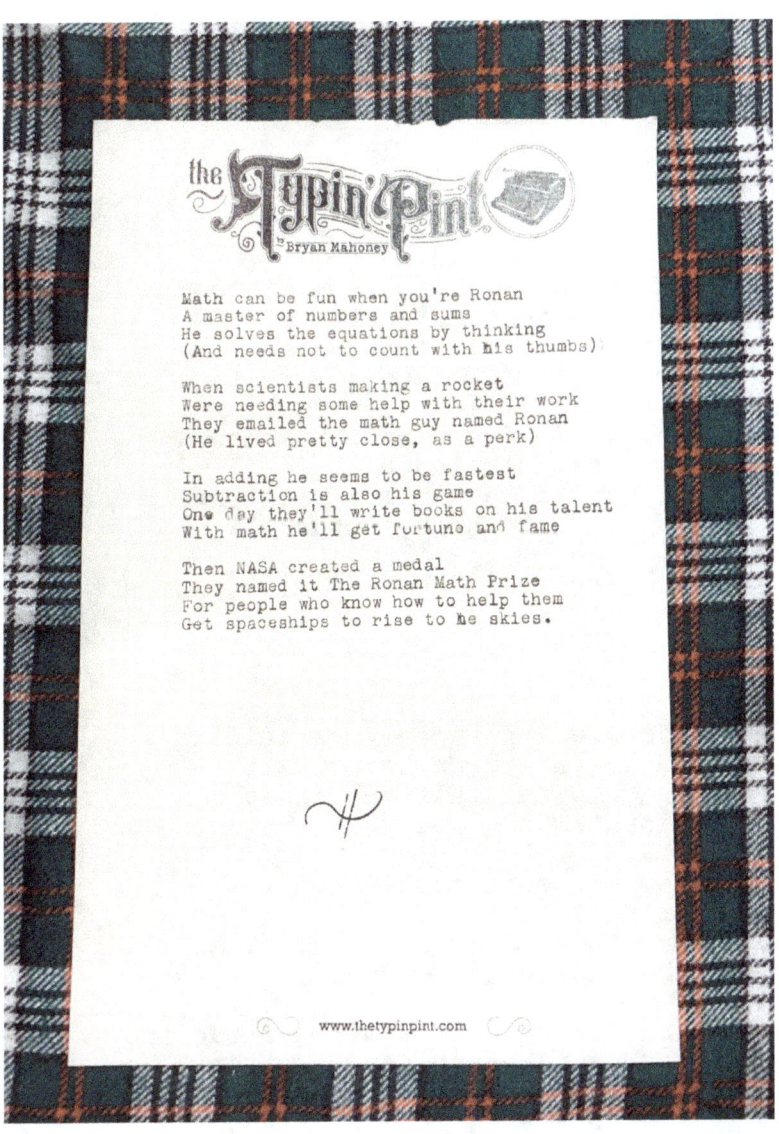

the **Typin' Pint**
by Bryan Mahoney

Math can be fun when you're Ronan
A master of numbers and sums
He solves the equations by thinking
(And needs not to count with his thumbs)

When scientists making a rocket
Were needing some help with their work
They emailed the math guy named Ronan
(He lived pretty close, as a perk)

In adding he seems to be fastest
Subtraction is also his game
One day they'll write books on his talent
With math he'll get fortune and fame

Then NASA created a medal
They named it The Ronan Math Prize
For people who know how to help them
Get spaceships to rise to he skies.

www.thetypinpint.com

BRYAN MAHONEY

There was a quote from Milton
Or Tennyson or Frost:
About the art of teaching,
"Not all who teach are lost"

The words I may have butcher'd
My poetry is loose
I learned hem in my schooling
(My path to here, obtuse)

The feeling's what's important;
Intent behind the words
A teacher had me hunt themlike
Acat that's tracking birds

When leadership's your calling
(especially for he young)
You know not all the impacts
Ofstatements fom your tongue

Your lessons makean imprint
Aripple in he world
New York is where it started,
Then influence unfurl'd

Your work built tow'rs of meaning
Your guidance blazed a light
Now face he world a student
And do what's feeling right.

the **Typin' Pint**

by Bryan Mahoney

The class was packed for a Wednesday
The final exams drawing near
The teacher could feel the excitement
Or was that a sweaty cold fear?

"Now nursing school isn't that easy,"
The teacher, named Jessica, said,
"But I'm here to help you with learning
(You'll all get to rest when you're
                                    dead)."

So Jessica started the lesson
A treatise on proper technique
To insert an IV directly
When patient's arm vein is a freak

The door to the classroom swung open;
A doctor swept fast 'cross the room
He needed a nurse - it's emergent
A janitor hurt by his broom

So Jessica joined him too quickly
The students had followed in suit
But when Jessica turned the corner
She saw a small table with fruit

#SURPRISE" yelled her colleagues &
                                    students,
And someone procured her a cake
For Jessica's birthday was coming
And these were the best friends to make

section 7   personal

1935 Smith Corona Sterling and 1941 Royal Companion.
Most of the poems in this book were written on these typewriters.

This book came about with the help of my ever-supporting wife and best nerd, Marcy Mahoney. Thank you for encouraging me to pursue my art in all its forms.

There are many people who helped me connect with the people I met in these poems. Thank you, friends at the International Printing Museum in Carson, California, who always provide me a spot to meet new people and tell their stories. For the same reasons, and for being a dear friend and for also taking care of my typewriters, thank you Aaron at Typewriter Connection.

For the friends and family who helped with prompts to help me practice, thank you: Laura, Kris, Erik(s), Daniel, Vi, Nia, Jack, Charlene, J4, Ian, Nic, Jay, Mark, and of course, Mom and Dad who are always supportive even if they don't always understand what it is I'm doing. That makes three of us.

All typewriter illustrations are by me, but three poems contain illustrations by Jay Shultz. We did these at DesignerCon in 2018 when we shared a booth. In our spare time, he'd draw a fantastical creature to which I would write a poem.

acknowledgments

I'd also like to acknowledge the mentorship and guidance of Robert Matson, who took a chance on a green college graduate and placed him on a newspaper beat in Canandaigua, N.Y. in May 2000. I've always tried to work as you worked, and set the same examples of leadership and friendship. And you gave me my first real job so this is kind of all your fault.

Want your own poem?

Order your own custom poem! Surprise Mom!
Let your cat know how you feel about him!

www.thetypinpint.com

art • design • writing